EXTRAORDINARY RECIPES FROM

WINE COUNTRY CHEF'S TABLE

ROY BREIMAN & LAURA SMITH BORRMAN
Photography by Rina Jordan

NAPA AND SONOMA

LP

LYONS PRESS
Guilford, Connecticut
An imprint of Globe Pequot Press

Lyons Press is an imprint of Globe Pequot Press.

All photography by Rina Jordan with the exception of the author photos on page 208 (top) by Jeff Caven Photography and (bottom) by Brian Ng.

Map by Alena Pearce © Morris Book Publishing, LLC

Editor: Katie Benoit
Project Editor: Tracee Williams
Text Design: Libby Kingsbury
Layout Artist: Nancy Freeborn

Library of Congress Cataloging-in-Publication data is available on file.

ISBN 978-0-7627-7928-4

Printed in the United States of America

10 9 8 7 6 5 4 3 2 1

Restaurants and chefs often come and go, and menus are ever-changing. We recommend you call ahead to obtain current information before visiting any of the establishments in this book.

To my wife, Pam, for her unwavering support—you are truly the most beautiful woman I've ever met. And to my mother, Jackie Baldwin, who taught me about visualization and manifestation—your guidance through the years has proven there are no dreams too big to accomplish through passion, commitment, and hard work. ~Roy Breiman

To my family for their love and support, especially my husband, Brandon, who is my greatest dining partner, my source of calm, and my inspiration each day. And to the chefs, winemakers, and farmers who allowed us to share their stories and recipes with all of you. ~Laura Smith Borrman

BERINGER VINEYARDS
Nevers
Medium + Toast
Toasted Heads
2009
TS-2
B09F3349

Contents

Acknowledgments

My deepest appreciation and acknowledgments go to Gerard Collet, Bernard Jacoby, Jean-Pierre Lortal, Bruno Tison, Christian Delouvier, Bruno Cirino, Dominique LeStanc, Paul Wolman, Armandino Batali, and Bill Harlan for their guidance, direction, and counsel over the years that allowed me the opportunity to expand my knowledge of culinary history, tradition, and craft both in the United States and Europe. I am indebted to the Pacific Northwest region for embracing us. Thank you, Yogi Hutsen, Scott Ostrander, and Peter LaFemina, for blessing the vision. Special credit goes to KC and the team in the bunker for making things happen and keeping everything on lockdown in my absence and to Mark Bodinet for his craftsmanship and our many inspired conversations. I am especially grateful to our agent, Rita Rosenkranz; our editor at Globe Pequot Press, Katie Benoit Cardoso; and cowriter Laura Smith Borrman for their genuine commitment and never-ending perseverance. And, finally, I want to express my sincere gratitude to the chefs, farmers, and artisans of Napa and Sonoma Counties who contributed their knowledge and skills, for without their collaborations and devotion to the pleasures of the table, this book would not have been possible.

—Roy Breiman

Thank you, first, to our editor, Katie Benoit Cardoso, for her positive reinforcement, constant flexibility, and enthusiastic appreciation of the details that bring these wine country stories to life.

Many thanks to our agent, Rita Rosenkranz, for her guidance and assistance with this opportunity.

To my project partners, Roy and Rina: We did it!

To Ed and Judy Hemmingsen, the charming proprietors of the lovely Belfast Bay Inn in Maine—your breakfasts and cheerful support made hours of writing in a "hotel room" more than tolerable. I got all the words . . .

To my corporate colleagues who knew I was working on a book in the off hours—thank you for your interest and excitement.

To my understanding friends, who sustained what felt like countless cancellations of plans and harried exchanges during this process—you're all awesome. Time for cocktails.

Huge thanks to my entire family, especially my parents, Calvin and Roberta Smith, for their enduring love and support and for all those weekends spent dog sitting while I traipsed around wine country. And to my sister, Emily Smith, for always bringing levity to overwhelming situations, encouraging and making me laugh from afar. Yo!

To Kevin Aguilar, a dear friend and brilliant writer whose love of stories and the personalities that make up the world around us will always inspire. You've left an indelible mark.

To my husband, Brandon, without whom I couldn't have done this or many other things. Thank you for eating with me when you weren't hungry, for your thoughtful feedback even when I disagreed, for being a pop culture savant, for your wisdom and gift with language, for your hundreds of hours in the car, for all the extra dishes you washed during my late nights of writing—and for always telling me I could do it. Life with you is spectacular.

Finally, to all the chefs, restaurateurs, food artisans, winemakers, and farmers who shared their stories, recipes, and delicious products with us. We are honored to be able to spread the word about you.

—Laura Smith Borrman

Introduction

Rolling hills covered in vineyards as far as the eye can see. Collections of cows grazing lazily on the few hillsides empty of grapes. Wildflowers bordering the country roads. And, of course, the wineries.

This is what most people know of the Napa and Sonoma Valleys of Northern California—that the area is responsible for some of the most incredible wines in the world. Red, white, or rosé; sparkling, dry, or sweet: From the renowned California cabernet sauvignon to beautiful zinfandels, pinot noirs, chardonnays, and many lesser known, lovely white varietals, it's the wine that made this region famous and still draws visitors the world over. But the food is just as incredible—and, in a way, is older than the wine.

Though the Napa and Sonoma regions offer the signature taste of California to locals and global jet-setters each day, California wine country's history is deeper than the wine tourism may indicate. Before there were vintners crawling the area, there were farmers and ranchers cultivating the land. Its diverse topography, ranging from the Mayacamas Mountains to the shores of Bodega Bay and the warm, arid valley of Dry Creek, presents a variety of agricultural possibilities. As a result, the region's rustic roots embody the story of immigrants searching for the American dream, and finding it through farming and offering up their harvest to the people of the area—and eventually, to those far beyond.

Native Americans, Russian settlers, Spanish explorers, and Italian immigrants are among those responsible for the region's early agricultural development, supplying seed varietals and planting wheat, apples, olives, grapes, cherries, pears, and plums, all still grown in the region today. Dairy farming and ranching has also been part of the valley picture for a long time, providing milk, cheese, butter, and all manner of meats, pork, and poultry to locals for more than a hundred years.

Throughout the twentieth century, the area's early agricultural abundance blossomed, with sweet corn, an array of squash varieties, heirloom tomatoes, and more stone fruits and berries, along with gorgeous local grains and legumes, including the famous "new world" Rancho Gordo beans, now endemic to the area. Gorgeous herbs are also grown throughout the region—lavender chief among them, its delicate buds covering the hills and heady fragrance permeating the air. Ranching has flourished as well, with popular pig and cattle farms spread across the valleys, along with goat, lamb, and turkey farms whose products make their way to dinner tables throughout the state and beyond. And, not to be overlooked, the area's close proximity to the Pacific Ocean brings succulent oysters, clams, a variety of fish, and the famous midwinter local favorite—fresh Dungeness crab—to tables throughout the region.

And the wine, of course, has been an evolving part of the valley picture from the beginning. Early immigrant families—with names like Mondavi, Tchelistcheff, Schram, and Niebaum—showed a commitment to the land from the start, farming it out of necessity and eventually out of what became an honored tradition. Many of these famous names are still producing—some have become a formidable presence in the world of food and wine—but now it is the children, grandchildren, and great-grandchildren who are tilling the land, growing the grapes, and producing what often seem like the most perfect expressions of wines one could imagine.

This unique blend of farming, fishing, ranching, and winemaking makes the Napa/Sonoma region a fantastic place to be a chef today. More than fifty are featured in the following pages of this book, each offering his or her take on delivering the area's special products to your plate.

ABOUT THE BOOK

Centered on the world's premier winemaking region and renowned culinary destination, *Wine Country Chef's Table* offers an intimate look at a region that thousands of travelers often just "taste." It is a regional cookbook and travelogue, offering gems of recipes along with restaurant, winery, and farm stories to both locals and visitors alike. In the book we feature great chefs, farmers, and food artisans from the distinct parts of the California wine country, spanning both the Napa and Sonoma Valleys.

Known the world over for its stellar wines and signature California landscapes, the Napa Valley is also a culinary star. "Like a modern-day Garden of Eden" is a phrase that comes up repeatedly when talking to chefs working in the area today, and it aptly describes the region's incredibly fertile soil that is responsible for such a long list of wonderful products.

Home to superchef Thomas Keller's palace of fine dining—The French Laundry—as well as ultracasual burger joint favorite, Gott's Roadside, and everything in between, California wine country is a veritable temple of culinary experiences. The region has been featured repeatedly on foodie TV, including Bravo's *Top Chef,* where finalists prepared a meal on the legendary Napa Valley Wine Train and served their specialties at a crush party. Many of the area's most famous chefs have even had television programs of their own.

At its heart, this book is about passion—a passion for life, for good food, for delicious wines, for freshly picked or harvested ingredients, and for gorgeous landscapes. It's about the unique culinary environment and agricultural bounty of an intensely popular part of the world. The book is a love letter to a region that many people have heard of or visited, but just a fortunate few truly know. It pays homage to the chefs, farmers, olive oil makers, and vintners who are devoted to the land and beautiful culinary products—and to sharing those products with people the world over.

Get a rare, intimate look at this famous locale by reading about the chefs and food artisans working there today and by preparing their special recipes. Whether it's breaking artisanal bread at Della Fattoria in Petaluma, sipping a glass of Morisoli zinfandel at Elyse in Napa, or sitting down to a Michelin-starred meal at Terra in St. Helena, we will journey together through the cultural richness of California's wine country. Get ready to taste the region through its recipes and the stories of the people that make it the incredible food and wine destination it is today.

We hope this book will give you a road map for your next trip to the region—or help you take a vicarious vacation through the stories of local chefs, winemakers, and food artisans who proudly present their work there each day. Bon appétit!

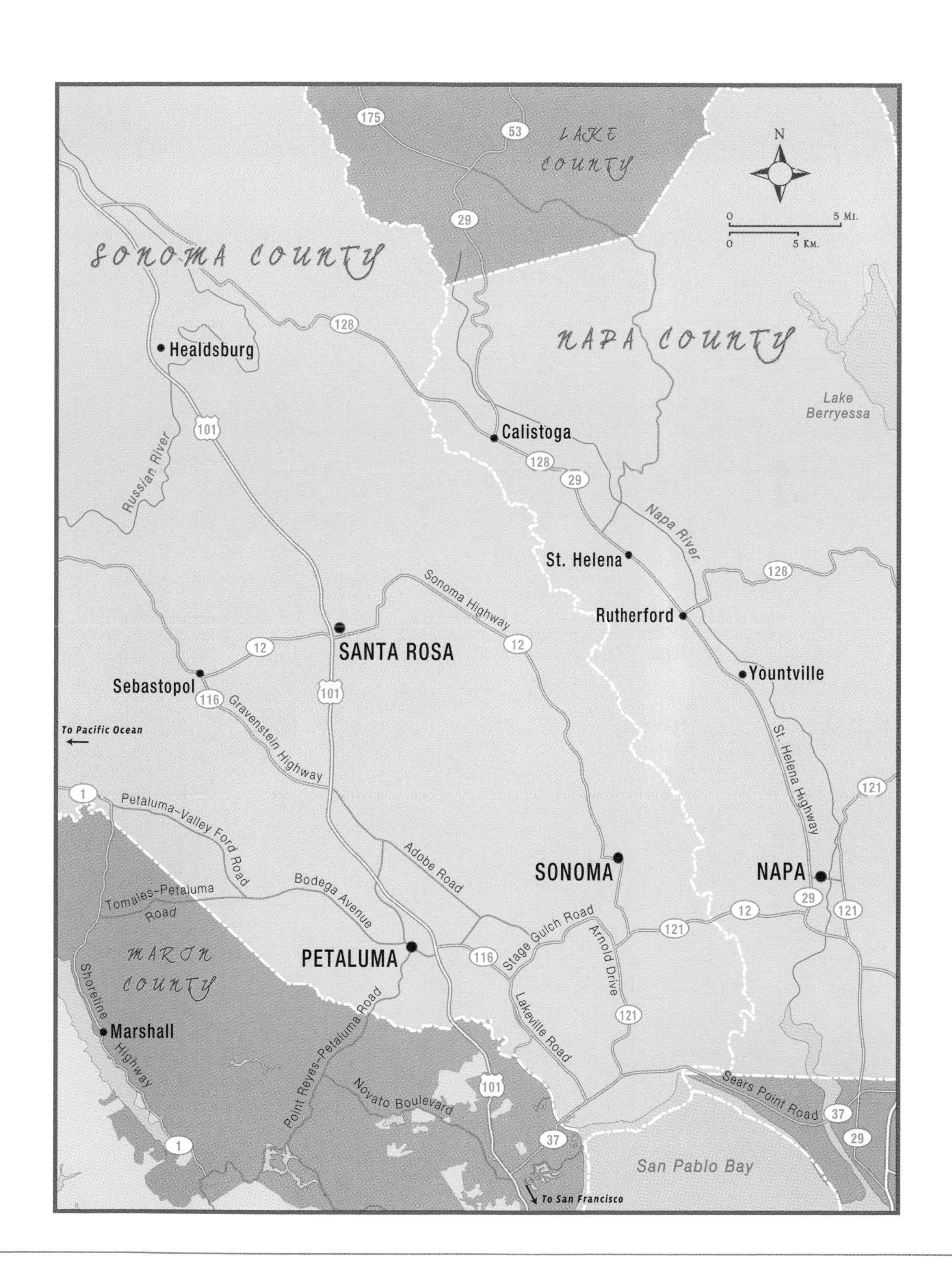
LAKE COUNTY
SONOMA COUNTY
NAPA COUNTY
MARIN COUNTY
N
0 5 MI.
0 5 KM.
Lake Berryessa
Healdsburg
Calistoga
Russian River
Napa River
St. Helena
Rutherford
Sonoma Highway
SANTA ROSA
Sebastopol
Yountville
Gravenstein Highway
To Pacific Ocean
St. Helena Highway
Petaluma-Valley Ford Road
Adobe Road
SONOMA
NAPA
Bodega Avenue
Tomales-Petaluma Road
Stage Gulch Road
Arnold Drive
PETALUMA
Shoreline Highway
Lakeville Road
Marshall
Point Reyes-Petaluma Road
Novato Boulevard
Sears Point Road
San Pablo Bay
To San Francisco
175
53
29
128
101
12
116
1
121
37

YOUNTVILLE

REGIONAL SPECIALTIES

Named posthumously for its founder, George Calvert Yount, a settler who laid the town boundaries in 1855, Yountville today is a tiny little town that is a must-visit on any trip to the Napa Valley. The town is known for its large US veterans community, a smattering of sophisticated hotels and markets, its designation as an American Viticultural Area (AVA) in the late 1990s, and its heady culinary stature as home to some of the most elite restaurants in the region.

Thomas Keller's venerated establishment, The French Laundry, which housed many local chefs who then went on to run their own successful restaurants, is the anchor of the town. But it's not the only revered Yountville spot. Two of Keller's more recent restaurants—Ad Hoc and Bouchon Bakery—are now destinations in their own right, drawing locals and visitors to experience a delightful taste of the region each day. Brix, a lovely restaurant with extensive on-site gardens, offers a taste of the region that has only improved over the years. And the newest member of the town's culinary family, Bardessono, offers a luxuriously relaxing experience with dining and lodging that still maintains a connection to its farming roots.

The amazing chefs from these restaurants—from Thomas Keller's chief leaders to others who are making a name for themselves in lesser known but equally stellar establishments—have graciously shared their recipes with us in this chapter. These "regional specialties" are so named for the way they represent the area's special farmland or a unique tradition at a particular restaurant. Some are simple, some are more complicated, but they are all very "wine country"—and all incredibly delicious.

AD HOC

6476 Washington Street
Yountville, CA 94599
(707) 944-2487
www.adhocrestaurant.com
Chef/Owner: Thomas Keller; Chef de Cuisine: Dave Cruz

Who could have imagined that a student of computer science and electrical engineering would one day be at the helm of one of a superchef's restaurants? Certainly not Dave Cruz, Texas native and original chef de cuisine of Thomas Keller's family-style establishment, Ad Hoc. Cruz grew up in a Philippine family in West Texas, and though he didn't dream of becoming a chef, he does remember a proud moment of cookery in the sixth grade.

"We were supposed to make something ourselves and bring it in to share with the class," Cruz explains. "I made the traditional Filipino dish, lumpia, and just remember walking in with a big tray of these crispy little rolls. It was pretty cool."

After attending college at the Polytechnic University of New York, working side jobs through school as a waiter to pay the bills, he became a computer systems engineer. But there was something he loved about cooking, and eventually he was drawn back to the kitchen. He calls working for the Thomas Keller Restaurant Group an amazing honor, and actually helped Chef Keller and then Executive Chef Jeffrey Cerciello develop and launch Ad Hoc.

Originally planned only as a temporary space, its casual-yet-still-stellar service and daily prix-fixe menu featuring classic comfort foods quickly became a hit. Locals and visitors alike clamored for this more accessible Thomas Keller culinary experience, one that didn't require two months' advance notice for reservations. And Cruz still loves it. He derives inspiration from traditional American dishes familiar to so many people—as well as conversations about food with his colleagues, friends, and guests.

Cruz relishes cooking from the shared gardens of the famous Keller collection of Yountville spots: The French Laundry, Bouchon, Bouchon Bakery (page 10), and Ad Hoc. His advice for home cooks who want to bring the Ad Hoc experience into their own kitchens is simple.

"There's a plaque in all of [Chef Keller's] restaurants, hanging just for the staff to see," Cruz divulges. "It contains a quote from Chef [Keller], which ends with 'to make people happy . . . that is what cooking is all about.'"

Marinated Skirt Steak

Recipe courtesy of Thomas Keller, excerpted from the *Ad Hoc at Home* cookbook, published by Artisan Books, 2009

(SERVES 6)

Skirt steak, part of the diaphragm, is a very flavorful cut. There are two sections of the skirt: an outside muscle and an inside muscle. The inside muscle is smaller, a little more uneven, and a little tougher than the outer skirt, which we prefer. The outer skirt is still a tough cut of meat and, because it's served medium-rare, not tenderized through long cooking, you need to slice it across the grain, straight down (thereby shortening the long muscle fibers that otherwise make it tough), to ensure it's tender. The marinade we use here, with abundant herbs and garlic, is excellent for all cuts of beef.

For the marinade:

6 thyme sprigs
2 (8-inch) rosemary sprigs
4 small bay leaves
1 tablespoon black peppercorns
5 garlic cloves, smashed, skin left on
2 cups extra-virgin olive oil

For the skirt steak:

6 (8-ounce) outer skirt steaks, trimmed of any silverskin
Kosher salt and freshly ground black pepper
Canola oil
2 tablespoons unsalted butter
4 thyme sprigs
2 garlic cloves, smashed, skin left on

Combine the thyme, rosemary, bay leaves, peppercorns, garlic, and olive oil in a medium saucepan and bring to a simmer over medium heat. Remove from the heat and let the marinade cool to room temperature.

Pull away the excess fat from the skirt steaks and discard. Put in a dish or a resealable plastic bag, add the marinade, and cover the dish or seal the bag, squeezing out excess air. Marinate for at least 4 hours, or for up to a day, in the refrigerator.

Remove the meat from the marinade and let sit at room temperature for about 30 minutes before cooking; discard the marinade. Dry the meat with paper towels. Season with salt and pepper.

Preheat oven to 350°F. Set a roasting rack in a roasting pan.

Heat some canola oil in a large frying pan over high heat. When it shimmers, add half the meat and quickly brown the first side. Turn the meat and, working quickly, add 1 tablespoon butter, 2 thyme sprigs, and 1 garlic clove and brown the meat on the second side, basting constantly; the entire cooking process should take only about 1½ minutes. Transfer the meat to the rack and spoon the butter, garlic, and thyme over the top. Wipe the pan and repeat with the remaining steaks.

Transfer the roasting pan to the oven and cook for 8–10 minutes, or until the center of the meat registers about 125°F. Remove from the oven and let the meat rest on the rack in a warm place for about 10 minutes for medium-rare.

Arrange the steak on a serving platter, or slice each piece against the grain, cutting straight down, and arrange on the platter. Garnish with the garlic and thyme.

Bardessono

6526 Yount Street
Yountville, CA 94599
(707) 204-6030
www.bardessono.com/restaurant_bar
Chef: Victor Scargle

A gorgeous Zen-like luxury property, Bardessono is a new member of the Napa Valley culinary community. Though the hotel, restaurant, and spa opened in 2009, its history goes back much further. Its location on the Bardessono family farmstead, which dates back to 1928, imbues the refined property with a subtle sense of history. Developer Phil Sherburne was actually specially selected by the family to design the property with minimal impact to the environment and the town of Yountville.

Chef Victor Scargle's self-described "West Coast Garden Cuisine" is a natural match for this blend of the modern and an honoring of the environment, and dining in his restaurant feels both elegant and earthy. Scargle's simple approach embraces classic artisanal values and stems from his upbringing in Santa Cruz County, where abalone, salmon, and squid are king. A University of California, Santa Barbara, finance and accounting graduate, he found it difficult over time to ignore his true calling in the kitchen. As he gradually acquired mentors such as Douglas Rodriguez, Traci Des Jardins, and Michael Mina, you can understand why.

When it comes to food, Scargle's philosophy is simple: Use what's in the garden, and the rest will take care of itself. If he can't get quite what he needs in the garden, he buys the best—and always handles ingredients with respect. Sixty-five percent of what he uses in the restaurant is grown on-site, and Scargle sources the remainder of his products from popular local farmers and ranchers, including Jim Reichardt for his famed Sonoma Liberty Ducks and Don Watson for lamb. He credits Des Jardins for much of what he learned about terroir and the importance of lovingly cultivated food.

Scargle's desire is to have a restaurant that's full of life, where you can see the garden on every plate; enjoy a relaxed, comforting experience; and discover the region's wines in a naturally educational way. In fact, wines are a major focus in the dining room, which has an understated elegance. Scargle works closely with Brett Fallows, the restaurant's director of wine, and the two create balanced pairings with unique varietals that work well with food. As the team describes it, "People are going to drink what they want to drink; our desire is to guide them toward a memorable experience that embodies the true inspiration that is the wine country."

Oven-Roasted Clucky Plucky Chicken with Garden Vegetable Tian, Basil Potato Puree & Marjoram Jus

(SERVES 6)

For the vegetable tian:

1 zucchini
1 Japanese eggplant
1 yellow squash
12 Sweet 100 tomatoes
12 Fino Verde basil leaves
2 Padron peppers, thinly sliced
Salt and pepper to taste
Extra-virgin olive oil to taste

For the marjoram jus:

4 shallots, thinly sliced
1 teaspoon coriander seeds
¼ teaspoon black peppercorns
1 teaspoon fennel seeds
1 bay leaf
6 parsley stems
2 tablespoons neutral oil
Salt to taste
1 cup white wine
3 cups chicken stock
1 bunch fresh marjoram
2 tablespoons butter

For the potato puree:

3 russet potatoes
½ cup butter
1½ cups heavy cream, heated
Pinch of kosher salt
2 Thai basil leaves, diced
2 Opal basil leaves, diced
2 Italian basil leaves, diced
5 Fino Verde basil leaves, diced

For the chicken and to plate:

6 (6-ounce) airline chicken breasts, drumstick and thigh attached
Kosher salt and pepper to taste
Neutral oil to taste
1¼ cups watercress, washed and stems removed
6 cherry tomatoes, cut in quarters
Extra-virgin olive oil to taste
2 tablespoons apple balsamic (Bates & Schmidt preferred); aged balsamic is a good substitute if apple is unavailable

Preheat oven to 350°F.

To make the vegetable tian, slice vegetables, Fino Verde basil leaves, and Padron peppers ⅛ inch thick and season with salt and pepper and extra-virgin olive oil. Layer vegetables in a staggered order in a 2-ounce aluminum cup or flan ring. Place in the preheated oven for 15–20 minutes. Remove and set aside, keeping warm.

To make the marjoram jus, place shallots and aromatics in a saucepot with oil. Season with salt and add white wine, then reduce by three-quarters. Add chicken stock, bring to a simmer, then reduce until the mixture just barely coats a spoon. Remove from heat, strain through a fine-mesh strainer, add marjoram, and steep for 20 minutes. Re-strain, then set aside.

To make the potato puree, peel and quarter potatoes and place them in cold, heavily salted water. Bring to a boil and cook potatoes until soft. Immediately remove and work through a food mill. Place potatoes back on low heat to dry out. Mix in butter

and hot cream with a spatula. Do not overmix or potatoes will become gluey. Keep warm.

To make the chicken, season with kosher salt on both sides and pepper on the non-skin side. Place skin-side down in a large, hot sauté pan with neutral oil (oil should be smoking before you place chicken in pan). Reduce heat to medium once all chicken breasts are in pan. Cook 80 percent on skin side (about 9 minutes), then turn over and cook another 5 minutes until juices run clear. Remove from pan and let rest 4 minutes.

Place tian in the oven to reheat. Place ¼ cup of potato puree in a small saucepan, heat through, and add basil leaves. On a large serving plate, place the puree and the tian.

Slice each chicken on an extreme bias—make 4 cuts to give you 5 pieces. Fan chicken around potatoes and tian. Toss watercress and cherry tomatoes in a little extra-virgin olive oil and apple balsamic and place on top of tian. Heat jus and finish with a little butter, whisk until well incorporated and spoon desired amount of jus in front of the chicken, not on the skin.

Milk-Fed Lamb with Lucy's Garden Vegetables, Saffron Spaetzle & Lemon Thyme Jus

(SERVES 6)

For the lamb:

6 (6-ounce) lamb T-bones, locally grown
6 (4-ounce) pieces lamb loin, locally grown
Kosher salt and black pepper to taste
2 tablespoons grapeseed oil
3 tablespoons butter
1 teaspoon lemon thyme leaves, stems removed
1 teaspoon sea salt, to finish the lamb

For the garden vegetables:

1 bunch torpedo onions, peeled and sliced
½ fennel bulb, medium dice
12 baby carrots
12 baby squashes, medium dice
1 baby yellow squash, medium dice
2 tablespoons olive oil
2 tablespoons butter
Kosher salt to taste

For the saffron spaetzle:

1 egg
1½ cups saffron water (small pinch of saffron steeped in 1½ cups hot water)
1⅛ cups white flour, organic
¼ bunch lemon thyme leaves
2 ounces grapeseed oil, for cooking spaetzle
Kosher salt to taste
Pinch of freshly ground black pepper

For the lemon thyme jus:

4 shallots, sliced
1 ounce grapeseed oil
¼ teaspoon coriander seeds
¼ teaspoon fennel seeds
1 bay leaf
6 parsley stems
2 cups white wine
2 quarts (8 cups) lamb or beef stock
1 bunch lemon thyme leaves
Kosher salt and black pepper to taste

Season the lamb with kosher salt on both sides and black pepper on one side; place in a hot pan with the grapeseed oil and lower heat to medium. For the T-bones, brown each side; turn over after 3–5 minutes on each side and remove from the pan. Quickly sear loins on both sides (approximately 3 minutes); remove and set aside, keeping warm. Place T-bones back in pan and add butter, over low heat, and lemon thyme and baste for an additional 5 minutes. Remove and let rest.

Place the vegetables in a sauté pan over medium-high heat with the olive oil and butter. Cook lightly for 5–7 minutes and season with salt. Set aside, keeping warm.

To make the spaetzle, thoroughly mix wet ingredients into dry ingredients. Let rest for 10–15 minutes.

Using a spaetzleater (like a box grater with a handle to push through) or a perforated hotel pan or colander with a rubber spatula, process spaetzle in small batches into salted boiling water. Once spaetzle floats, remove from the boiling water and shock in ice water. Remove and place on a perforated pan to remove excess water.

To finish spaetzle, place 2 ounces grapeseed oil in a pan over medium-high heat until hot and add spaetzle. Sauté spaetzle until crispy and golden brown; drain on a paper towel.

To make the jus, place shallots in a saucepot with 1 ounce grapeseed oil, along with coriander, fennel, bay leaf, parsley, and a pinch of salt. Caramelize lightly and add white wine; reduce by three-quarters and add stock. Bring to a simmer and add lemon thyme. Skim and simmer for 15 minutes; adjust flavor with kosher salt and pepper.

To serve, plate the roasted vegetables and crispy spaetzle. Place the T-bone on the vegetables and slice the loin piece on the bias, making 4 cuts (to result in 5 slices). Fan the slices in a semicircle around the spaetzle. Sauce the plate in front of lamb, not over the top, and sprinkle sea salt on top of the lamb.

Bouchon Bakery

6528 Washington Street
Yountville, CA 94599
(707) 944-2253
www.bouchonbakery.com/yountville
Chef/Owner: Thomas Keller; Head Baker: Matt McDonald

Like a taste of California and Paris rolled into one, Bouchon Bakery offers a beautifully delicious array of pastries, tender-crisp French macarons, classic American cookies, traditional baked goods, delicate chocolates, savory quiches, and, of course, incredible bread. The latter is the reason the bakery first opened its doors: It was established to supply its revered neighbor, The French Laundry, with great bread.

"I always remembered the bread at a restaurant," shares certified master baker Matt McDonald, who runs the bread operation at Thomas Keller's original Yountville bakery—now also with outlets in New York City, Las Vegas, and Beverly Hills. "For me, if the bread was great, it sealed the deal."

And for the Southern California kid who began his baking career as a dishwasher in his family's donut shop, working as part of Keller's team still sometimes feels like a dream.

"It's incredible, like I'm on the all-star team," says McDonald. It is amazing to learn that someone who was on the Bread Bakers Guild of America Baking Team that placed in the international finals in both 1999 and 2002 "wanted to run and hide from the bakery business" as a teenager.

McDonald never imagined pursuing a career in what was his family's business, but after several years in college, he had an epiphany. "I thought money would be the most important thing," he explains. "But I gradually realized it was really cool to be able to go to work and look forward to it." So he began to seriously pursue baking, working in his mother's bakery in Eureka. He never entered a full culinary school program, but always challenged himself in the off-hours to learn different styles of bread making, including the California classic, sourdough. His career evolved and took him to a class at The Culinary Institute of America in St. Helena, where he met his future wife, and eventually to Keller. And the rest, as they say, is history.

"Food is my life. It's really awesome to be in a place where food is appreciated like it is here."

The thing he values most about Bouchon Bakery is its accessibility: "Everyone can connect with a bakery." McDonald is careful to say that the pizza recipe on page 12 (which was born when the bakery started making pizza for the family meal at The French Laundry, with staff members carrying it down the street) is not a fancy, fine-dining version of the Italian—and American—classic.

"Our pizza is my memory of what I liked about pizza when I was a child—the crust is thicker, fluffier, and crispy all at once," he shares. The bakery team makes its own sauce and ricotta, and uses many ingredients from its own farm. "But the pepperoni is what people love most—it always goes first."

Bacon-Cheddar Breadsticks

(SERVES 4–6)

Chef recommends weighing ingredients for consistency.

For breadsticks:

1½ cups (12.4 ounces) grated cheddar cheese
5 tablespoons (2.5 ounces) bacon fat
3 cups (24.7 ounces) flour
1½ cups (12.4 ounces) water
4½ teaspoons (0.5 ounce) yeast
3⅓ teaspoons (0.6 ounce) salt

For egg wash:

1 egg, beaten with one tablespoon water or milk

Melt the cheddar and bacon fat in a pot, stirring continuously until uniform and liquid in consistency.

Place all the ingredients in a mixing bowl; be sure to pour the wet ingredients over the dry ingredients. With a dough hook, mix on low speed until incorporated, approximately 4 minutes. Increase the speed to medium and mix for 10 minutes. Allow the dough to rest for 15 minutes.

Flatten out dough and wrap in plastic wrap. Chill until firm, about 1 hour.

Roll dough to ⅛ inch thick and cut into desired shape. Cover with a clean dish towel and proof (let sit in a warm place to rise) for 1 hour at room temperature. The dough is ready to bake when it leaves a depression after pressed.

Preheat oven to 350°F. Brush with egg wash and bake for approximately 13 minutes.

Pizza Dough

(SERVES 4–6; YIELDS 3 HALF-SHEET PANS OF PIZZA)

Chef recommends weighing ingredients for consistency.

3 pounds flour
1¼ cups (10 ounces) sugar
2¼ teaspoons (0.25 ounce) yeast
5 teaspoons (1 ounce) salt
3⅔ cups (29 ounces) water
5 tablespoons extra-virgin olive oil

Special equipment:

Half-sheet pans
Olive oil spray
Rolling pin

Procedure for day one of two days:

Place all the dry ingredients in a mixing bowl. Add the wet ingredients. With a dough hook, mix on low speed until it is well combined, then mix on medium speed for 14 minutes. Set aside and let the dough rest for 15 minutes.

Divide the dough into 25.5-ounce pieces; this should yield 3 pieces. Wrap the dough in plastic wrap and place in the refrigerator overnight.

Procedure for day two of two:

Preheat oven to 450°F.

Spray the half-sheet pans with olive oil. Process each piece of dough one at a time. On a lightly floured surface, roll out the first round of dough with a rolling pin to fit a half-sheet pan (make sure it fits up the sides of the sheet pan). Repeat with each other piece of dough, for three half-sheet pans total.

Apply the desired sauce, cheese, and toppings to your taste to each half-sheet of dough. Bake in the preheated oven until the crust is golden brown, approximately 25 minutes. (As many home ovens may not fit more than one half-sheet pan at a time, keep the other two dressed and in the fridge—but bake right away.)

Brix

7377 St. Helena Highway
Yountville, CA 94558
(707) 944-2749
www.brix.com
Chef: Chris Jones; Owners: The Kelleher Family

Brix feels like a wrapped gift, tucked away in a secret garden yet still in the open. Set on sixteen gorgeous acres, the restaurant naturally draws inspiration from its vegetable and flower gardens, fruit and citrus orchards, and vineyards. And chef Chris Jones, who has worked at popular restaurants throughout the region, is a natural fit to lead the kitchen.

Jones was enamored with the kitchen at a young age. Eventually a California Culinary Academy graduate, his first food memories are of tilling the home garden after the example set by his family, which was full of farmers. The connection between food and region, he says, is inspiring.

Jones's daily changing, farm-to-table menu at Brix stems from that childhood desire—to "cook with what's in the field" and to have a restaurant that's fun at the same time. Though he has cooked in Washington, DC, and Chicago—where he fell in love with French and Italian techniques—it's in the California wine country where he feels most at home. Perhaps it's the kindred spirit he feels with local farmers and winemakers, and the fixation on local, incredible ingredients that seems so common in this part of the world.

Jones also works closely with the restaurant's sommelier, Jeff Cramer, who has produced an amazing, standout wine list of unique and diverse offerings. It boasts more than 800 bottles, including hard-to-find selections as well as a one-of-kind Oakville cabernet sauvignon collection.

When it comes to artisan craftsmanship, Jones provides an exemplary model at Brix: He makes his own charcuterie, cheese, sausage, and pasta and is experimenting with drying chilies and making mustards. He fosters a dynamic, educational environment that is not stuffy or overwrought, which feels special in today's food-obsessed world. When he's not practicing whole-animal butchery or making his own products, you may find him playing boules or riding his '66 Vespa. His outlook on running a restaurant in wine country is simple: "It's the people and the region that make up the story of my cuisine, and for that I'm truly grateful."

Warm Pacific Oysters, Leek Confit, Salmon Caviar & Vermouth Cream

(SERVES 6)

For the oysters:

36 medium Pacific oysters

For the leek confit:

4 medium leeks
¼ cup unsalted butter
Salt and white pepper

For the vermouth cream:

1 whole shallot
1 tablespoon unsalted butter
1 cup dry white vermouth
All the reserved oyster liquor
2 thyme sprigs
1 bay leaf
3 whole white peppercorns
1 cup heavy cream
Picked herbs to garnish (parsley, chive, chervil, and tarragon)
1 ounce (2 tablespoons) salmon caviar to garnish

Holding an oyster in a kitchen towel with the larger half of the shell on a secure work surface, insert the tip of your knife into the soft area at the hinge of the oyster and gently apply pressure in a downward motion until the knife penetrates into the oyster. Gently separate the oyster from the muscle that attaches it to the shell, and place it in a bowl. Pour the oyster liquor through a fine-mesh sieve over the oyster in the bowl. Repeat with the rest of the oysters, then refrigerate and reserve.

To make the confit, separate the dark green portion of leaves from the leeks. Remove the root end and slit the leeks in half lengthwise. Wash thoroughly between the leaves and small dice the entire white portion. Place the diced leeks in a cool sauté pan with the butter and slowly increase the heat of the pan until the leeks begin simmering. Season with salt and pepper and slowly cook the leeks until tender. Remove the confit from the pan and reserve.

To make the cream, dice the shallot and sauté it in the butter until soft. Add the vermouth and reduce it until it is almost dry. Add the oyster liquor, thyme, bay leaf, and peppercorns. Bring the mixture to a boil, reduce the heat, and add the heavy cream. Simmer until slightly thickened and season with salt. Pass through a fine-mesh sieve.

To plate, gently heat the vermouth cream and add the oysters and leek confit until the oysters are just cooked. Arrange 6 oysters each and equal portions of the leek and cream mixture in warmed shallow dishes and garnish with the mixed herbs and salmon caviar. Serve with toasted brioche.

Chardonnay-Braised Pork Osso Bucco with Creamy Polenta, Broccoli Rabe & Horseradish Gremolata

(SERVES 6)

For the pork:

6 Niman Ranch pork osso bucco or all-natural pork shanks
Salt and black pepper
¼ cup olive oil
1 yellow onion, quartered
2 celery stalks
1 small carrot, peeled
4 cups chardonnay
4 garlic cloves, crushed
4 thyme sprigs
1 bay leaf
5 black peppercorns
2 quarts (8 cups) pork or chicken stock

For the polenta:

2 cups water
2 cups milk
Salt and white pepper to taste
1 cup polenta
¼ cup unsalted butter
¼ cup mascarpone cheese
½ cup grated Parmesan cheese

For the broccoli rabe:

3 bunches broccoli rabe, tough stems removed
2 tablespoons unsalted butter
2 garlic cloves, thinly sliced
Salt and white pepper to taste

For the gremolata:

1 bunch Italian flat-leaf parsley, cleaned from the stems and finely chopped
Juice and zest of 2 lemons
2 garlic cloves, finely minced
2 tablespoons fine bread crumbs
2-inch peeled horseradish root, grated
Sea salt to taste

Heavily season the shanks with salt and black pepper. Meanwhile, heat a large sauté pan over medium heat and add the olive oil. When the oil is very hot, place the shanks in the pan and sear until browned on all sides.

Preheat oven to 350°F.

In a braising pan, add the vegetables for the braise and the chardonnay. Bring to a boil and reduce until almost dry. Add the seared shanks to the braising pan, then add the spices and the stock to just cover the shanks. Bring the entire mixture to a simmer. Cover the braising pan with aluminum foil and place in the preheated oven. Cook for 1–1½ hours or until the shanks are just fork tender.

Remove the braising pan from the oven and cool to room temperature. Carefully remove the shanks from the braising liquid. Pass the braising liquid through a fine-mesh sieve and skim any fat from the top of the stock.

In a large saucepan, bring the braising liquid to a boil, reduce to a simmer, and skim off any fat that forms on the top. Reduce by half to a slightly thickened consistency.

To make the polenta, add the water and milk to a medium saucepan and season with salt and white pepper to taste. Bring the liquid to a simmer. While stirring with a wire whisk slowly add the polenta and beat into the liquid. Simmer and continue to stir for approximately 30–40 minutes or until the polenta has thickened and lost most of its "bite." Beat in the butter and mascarpone and Parmesan cheeses, and adjust the seasoning. Cover and keep warm.

To make the broccoli rabe, bring a large pot of salted water to boil. Blanch the broccoli rabe until tender, then shock in ice water until cool and drain. Heat the butter in a large sauté pan over medium-low heat until melted. Add the garlic and sauté until translucent, then add the blanched broccoli rabe, season to taste, and heat till warm.

To make the gremolata, mix the parsley, lemon juice and zest, garlic, bread crumbs, and grated horseradish. Season with sea salt.

To plate, preheat oven to 400°F. In a large sauté pan, reheat the pork shanks together with the reduced braising liquid in the preheated oven, basting the sauce over the shanks occasionally as they heat, for approximately 10 minutes or until they are hot in the center. Spoon the warmed polenta into the center of 6 heated bowls, evenly distribute the sautéed broccoli rabe on top of the polenta, and top with a braised pork shank each. Cover each osso bucco with the reduced sauce and garnish with the horseradish gremolata.

HEALDSBURG

STARTERS

Stylish and refined, Healdsburg feels like the place where the jet-setters go when they visit California wine country. Its town square is small, pretty, and lined with sophisticated boutiques, galleries, wineries, and restaurants, some of them of the celebrity and Michelin-starred variety. And its wine is revered—pinot noir is the king of noble grapes in this area, also famous for its zinfandels and chardonnays. Nearby Dry Creek, Russian River, and Alexander Valley appellations produce fruit that feeds the passion of local winemakers, who transform that fruit into some of the greatest wines in the world.

With that lofty status, one might be surprised that Healdsburg is also surprisingly down to earth. Along with its boutiques and fine wines are old-fashioned candy shops, bookstores, and a twice-weekly farmers' market that, while petite, rivals some of the best in the country with its variety (founded in 1978, it was one of the original "certified farmers' markets" in the state). Families patronize the market and stroll the streets along with the tourists, and the town's restaurants see as many regulars as they do visitors.

Situated in one of the northernmost parts of the region and considered to have soil that is among the best for agriculture, Healdsburg and its surrounding territory is home to dozens of small farms. And all of them seem to have close and longstanding relationships with the town's chefs, who are zealots when it comes to fresh produce and local sourcing, making for a fabulous dining experience.

Whether it's visiting its more than one hundred area wineries and tasting rooms or pulling up a chair and a book at one of its many European-inspired cafes, Healdsburg offers a lovely, very civilized, and simultaneously unpretentious wine country experience for the visitor—who may just decide to stay and become a "townie."

Bistro Ralph

109 Plaza Street
Healdsburg, CA 95448
(707) 433-1380
www.bistroralph.com
Chef/Owner: Ralph Tingle

Ralph Tingle did not plan to be a chef. He was living in Aspen in the 1970s and simply wanted to ski during the day, so he took a job as a dishwasher at the local steak house. Then he was confronted with a fateful decision: to be a busboy or the broiler's assistant. He chose the kitchen. It was from those humble beginnings that his career in restaurants was born—and the impromptu plan has paid off, as he now celebrates twenty years at his eponymous eatery, Bistro Ralph.

Originally from Southern California, Tingle is now a fixture in the Healdsburg community—and a relaxed guy who quickly feels like someone you've known all your life. A devotee of Burning Man and a former resident of some of the most vibrant, artistic cities in the world, including Paris, New York, Los Angeles, and Santa Fe, Tingle opened his restaurant in 1992 after pondering where in the world he really wanted to live. He chose California wine country as the perfect match for his wine-loving sensibilities (his parents even bottled their own wine when he was a kid).

Though he's worked in intense, renowned fine-dining environments and appreciates the artistry and talent they foster, Tingle describes his own food as straightforward and simple. "I don't like overly touched cuisine," he says, and is most awed by peasant food. He is fervent about using local ingredients. "Without knowing it, I was all about 'local' twenty years ago," he reflects.

His own menu is a fantastic example of this love, a mishmash of the best dishes from a variety of cuisines, weighted toward the French, along with many of his own creations. Importantly, the menu relies on the finest local products: Tingle insists even his wine come from not just Sonoma or Napa Counties, but Healdsburg specifically. Dark, rich, hearty, and transportive, his chicken livers are addictive, to be enjoyed with friends and a bracing glass of white wine. A buttery halibut-cheek special—served with fresh spinach and cherry tomatoes—tastes like lobster. And the Plate of 1000 Fries and the Bistro Sundae Animal Style—served with chocolate sauce, caramel, and locally made toffee—are like stoner dream-food.

Tingle loves his "great local clientele" who patronize the bistro's thirteen tables and single counter, and enjoys "flying under the radar"—being steadfast in his success without being showy or fancy. One thing's for certain: If you hang out with Chef Ralph and his team for lunch, dinner, or even Sunday brunch, you'll get the insider's wine country experience, and you'll fall in love with chicken livers.

Bistro Ralph's Chicken Livers

(SERVES 4 AS AN APPETIZER OR 1 AS AN ENTREE)

Try to use fresh livers from your butcher. Organic is even better. We find that they need to be cooked on high heat to properly caramelize them. Cook them through, but overcooking renders them dry. At the restaurant we sauté each order in its own individual pan to be able to sear the livers properly. They are in and out of the pan in three minutes. Enjoy!

½ pound fresh chicken livers
2 tablespoons olive oil to coat pan
1 tablespoon sweet butter, divided (use half to sauté with and half to finish dish)
½ yellow onion, sliced and caramelized (caramelize by sautéing onion slices in a pat of butter and bit of olive oil over high heat in a small sauté pan until the onion takes on a golden brown color)
2 tablespoons rendered pancetta lardons (okay to substitute bacon; note that it's smokier)
1 tablespoon chopped mixed herbs (sage, thyme, oregano, parsley)
¼ cup balsamic vinegar
¼ cup veal demi-glace
Salt and pepper to taste

Trim excess fat from livers while your sauté pan is warming on a high burner. Use a pan just big enough to have livers in one layer.

Once the pan is hot, add olive oil to it. When it begins to smoke, add ½ tablespoon of butter. This technique helps the liver caramelize. Immediately add livers and shake pan to spread livers to one layer.

Let the pan do the cooking and don't move livers until edges become pink, which is your hint to turn them over. Once livers have been turned, add onions and pancetta. Simmer for about 15 seconds to heat up onions and pancetta, then add herbs and deglaze pan with balsamic vinegar. Reduce by half and add veal demi-glace. Briefly reduce, season to taste, and swirl in other ½ tablespoon of butter.

Remove from heat and serve in a warm bowl or plate. We like to serve some fried polenta as an accompaniment. A salad works well, too.

Bistro Ralph's Chicken Paillard with Brown Butter, Lemon & Capers

(SERVES 1)

The Chicken Paillard has been on the Bistro's lunch and dinner menu forever. Our biggest seller is a delicious peasant dish; I still enjoy it after twenty years. It is a versatile dish that will accommodate just about any side dish from a salad to potatoes or wilted greens . . . and a glass of wine.

1 (8-ounce) chicken breast, best quality (boneless and skinless)
½ cup unseasoned bread crumbs
Scant ¼ cup dried polenta (creating a 1-to-3 ratio with bread crumbs)
Salt and black pepper
¼ cup sweet butter
1 large tablespoon capers, rinsed (the smaller the better, and packed in salt)
1 lemon, juiced and zested (zest in strands or grated)

Place the trimmed chicken breast between two layers of plastic wrap and use a mallet to pound it uniformly ¼ inch thick.

Mix the bread crumbs and polenta and put on a plate or pie dish. Season the pounded breast with salt and pepper and lay it into the breading on both sides.

Preheat an 8-inch sauté pan on high heat. The pan must be very hot to start with. This dish cooks in a hurry. You must have everything ready: capers, lemon juice, and lemon zest. Once the pan is hot, add butter and let it melt and bubble before you add the breaded chicken. Be careful not to splash the butter onto you; that doesn't feel good.

The heat should remain on high. The butter needs to be browned. Turn over the chicken breast after the edge turns a lighter color; the underside of the breast should be golden brown. When the butter is brown, add the capers to the butter, not on top of the chicken.

After 15 seconds or so, the chicken should be cooked. At that point, add the lemon juice and zest. Remove the paillard from the pan and place on a warmed plate. Pour the sauce over the top and you're ready to eat.

Chopped Italian parsley is nice on top, but feel free to play with the presentation, like adding green onion, garlic, shallots, an herb, peppers.

Costeaux French Bakery

417 Healdsburg Avenue
Healdsburg, CA 95448
(707) 433-1913
www.costeaux.com
Owners/Operators: The Seppi Family: Nancy and Karl Seppi
General Manager: Will Seppi

The popularity of vintage posters and black-and-white photographs these days makes them easy to dismiss. But look closely at the few hanging on the walls of Costeaux French Bakery: The stories behind them are real. And they reveal the incredible history of bread making, honored with countless awards, linked to this fantastic bakery-cafe.

Originally founded in 1923 as The French American Bakery, Costeaux has blossomed over the years, the last thirty under the insightful eye of the Seppi family. The photographs behind the counter show the generations of baking that have brought delicious breads—including the original two (sweet and sour French), a delightfully hearty multigrain, and a unique, addictive take on ciabatta—to the Healdsburg community. Some people swear by their sandwich rolls and buns, while others like to pull up a chair in the cafe for a generous slice of incredible, golden-brown-topped quiche and a cup of coffee. But, back to those awards.

The first for the Seppi family—for its sourdough deli roll—is memorialized with a poster from the 1981 Sonoma County Fair. Nancy and Karl Seppi won it just six months after buying the bakery, a decision that would change the course of their, and their children's, lives forever.

They didn't plan on having a bakery, but when asked by a great-aunt if they'd be interested in buying the nearly fifty-year-old business that was for sale, they jumped at the chance. Now their son, Will, is the consummate host and general manager of the business, which extends beyond the walls of the bakery-cafe into wholesale, supplying many of the area's popular restaurants with their bread-basket contents to start the meal.

The Seppi kids grew up in the business, answering phones, sweeping the floors, washing dishes—"and when we knew all of that, we could wait on customers," Will remembers. A former accountant, Will was drawn back to the family business at the encouragement of his parents and by a realization that he and his own family yearned for a simpler life, focused on all the best things. "There's nothing wrong with having a little wine, a piece of good cheese, and great bread every day," he says, smiling.

Will is also immensely proud of the bakery's history as a family business. As a matter of fact, the original owner's great-grandson works the cafe's floors today as a server—keeping tradition alive and bellies full with the "staple of life." Will wants customers to feel like guests in his own home, "eating a meal that my family made, sitting around the table together." He invites you to linger as long as you like.

Focaccia

(SERVES 8–10)

2 cups bread flour
¼ teaspoon salt
2 teaspoons olive oil
¾ cup milk
1 (¼-ounce) package fresh active yeast, crumbled

Salt to taste
Olive oil to taste
Optional toppings to taste: rosemary, lavender, sun-dried tomatoes, goat cheese, olives

Combine first five ingredients. Mix together by hand or stand mixer (with dough hook) for 8–12 minutes until developed. Finish by hand, on a lightly floured surface, kneading dough until smooth. Place in a bowl covered with plastic or cloth in a warm spot (preferably 75 to 90-plus degrees). Let dough double in size.

Preheat oven to 400°F.

After dough has doubled, remove from bowl and divide in half. Place each piece on a sheet pan or pizza stone. Flatten and dimple dough with your hands and fingers to yield 2 approximately 10-inch rounds. Brush with olive oil and top with a salt of your choice. Add rosemary, lavender, or other herbs and toppings such as sun-dried tomatoes, goat cheese, and olives.

Bake in the preheated oven until done (approximately 30–40 minutes depending on your oven, baking environment, and skill set). Note: If the crust turns black, it's probably done!

Focaccia makes for a wonderful sandwich bread. Cut in half and fill with your favorite accoutrements.

DaVero

766 Westside Road, Healdsburg, CA 95448
(707) 431-8000 · www.davero.com
Owners: Ridgely and Colleen McGlynn

Craftsmanship meets a love of agriculture amidst olive groves and stone fruit orchards at DaVero farm and winery—and it is where Ridge (as he likes to be called) and Colleen McGlynn have made their home since 1982. What began as a weekend retreat property in the mid-1980s has grown into a full-production, certified biodynamic farm, producing premier olive oils and natural yeast fermentation wines.

Passionate about finishing oils, Ridge traveled to Italy and was inspired by 800-year-old olive trees at Fattoria Mansi Bernardini, a farm outside of Lucca, and was fortunate to bring cuttings from those special trees back home. The cuttings took root and have since paved the way for the production of unique, award-winning olive oils previously unparalleled on US soil.

DaVero became the first and only US olive oil to win a blind tasting of Tuscany oils, when Mario Batali snuck it into a private tasting by the Gambero Rosso panel, an esteemed Italian judging board, at his New York restaurant, Babbo. DaVero's 1998 Dry Creek Estate was, to the delight of its makers and surprise of the panel, the clear winner.

The McGlynns treat their farm as an organism, under the premise "healthy farm, healthy crop." In addition to wine and olive oils, they also make delicious preserves, jams, and vinegars from the farm's crops—underscoring the farm's spectacular bounty.

As youngsters, the couple seemed destined for farm ownership one day. Ridge always had an affinity for Italy—and his early experience with learning about Italian cuisine and "eating close to the earth" stayed with him. Colleen grew up on a farm in Wisconsin, as part of a family of ten who only ate what they grew. She went on to become a chef, working with Jeremiah Tower at his famous Stars restaurant in San Francisco before eventually making her way up the coast in search of better weather.

What is important to note about DaVero's (and other) olive oils is that different varietals have different levels of brightness. The McGlynns advise matching oils to your use—seek extra-virgin for cooking—and tasting for good fruit flavors, a pleasing viscosity, and mouth feel. As a guide, Ligurian oils tend to be lighter with a fuller fruit flavor, while Tuscan oils are robust and peppery. French styles tend to be more delicate, with a hint of spice, and southern Italian are very robust—perfectly suited for the cuisine of that region. When it comes to healthful properties, greener oils are higher in the natural antioxidant polyphenol.

Restaurant at Madrona Manor

1001 Westside Road
Healdsburg, CA 95448
(800) 258-4003
www.madronamanor.com/restaurant.htm
Executive Chef: Jesse Mallgren

Nestled in the foothills of Healdsburg, amidst olive trees and stone fruit orchards, lies the historic retreat Madrona Manor. Built in 1881, the manor's Victorian styling brings you back to the height of wine country elegance. The property's eight acres of gardens are spectacular, creating a perfect balance of historical surroundings and outstanding local, seasonal cuisine, discovered by residents and wine travelers alike.

A dedication to sourcing and offering a truly memorable dining experience has led to Michelin-star recognition for the Restaurant at Madrona Manor. And its chief for the last eleven years, executive chef Jesse Mallgren, has played a huge role in earning the restaurant this distinction. A Sonoma County native, Mallgren's quiet intensity has brought together his various influences—his mother's passion for exotic cooking and his own experience working for such California culinary icons as Jeremiah Tower and Gary Danko—in a focused way at the helm of Madrona Manor.

Mallgren uses local farmers, trusts his palate, and is self-taught. Inspired by his past experiences with foraging and artisan bread making, he creates what he calls "new California cuisine," highlighting products from the manor's organic garden. His experience in Aspen, where he "had to fly in everything," makes him truly appreciate the incredible products he now has at his fingertips. He buys raw milk and cream to make cultured buttermilk and fresh butter for the restaurant, and believes in a simple approach—creating memorable flavor profiles with the best local products, giving guests the best of what each season has to offer.

Mallgren seems to have passed down his special, delicate touch and appreciation for the finest ingredients to the next generation as well: His young son, Wiley, can identify herbs by name in the garden—and was once found wrapping basil around a tomato for a snack.

Garden Pole Bean Salad

(SERVES 4)

You may substitute haricots verts or any summer green bean for the pole beans. It is also nice to use half green and half yellow for a color contrast. I like to serve this salad at the height of summer when the bean plants produce the most and the sugar content of the beans is at its highest point. If you want, you may turn this into a lunch entree by adding a piece of grilled ahi tuna.

1 pound green or yellow beans
2 large egg yolks
1 small garlic clove
1 baby red beet, cooked and peeled
½ cup olive oil (not extra-virgin)
¼ cup cabernet vinegar (or any other good-quality vinegar), reduced to ½ tablespoon
Salt and freshly ground black pepper to taste
1 teaspoon freshly chopped chives
12 thin slices Parmigiano-Reggiano
12 thin slices summer truffles (optional)

Cook the beans to al dente in boiling water and refresh under cold water. Set aside.

Combine egg yolks, garlic, and cooked red beet in food processor. Slowly add olive oil to make a mayonnaise, add reduced vinegar, and season to taste.

Toss beans with 2 tablespoons of the mayonnaise, taste for seasoning.

Divide dressed beans on the center of 4 plates. Sprinkle chopped chives on top of beans and top with shaved cheese. Finish with freshly shaved summer truffles.

Wild Salmon "Confit a la Minute" with Baby Shiitake Mushrooms, Zucchini Blossoms, Zucchini & Cucumber Flowers

(SERVES 4)

For the shiitake mushroom and zucchini ragout:

½ cup (3.5 ounces) baby shiitake mushrooms, stems removed
2 teaspoons butter
1 teaspoon finely diced shallot
¼ teaspoon salt
¼ cup (1.5 ounces) finely diced zucchini
2 thinly sliced zucchini blossoms
Pinch of chopped chives (about 2 whole chives)

For the carrot foie gras sauce:

1.6 ounces foie gras
Kosher salt
Extra-virgin olive oil
1⅛ cups fresh carrot juice
¼ teaspoon lemon juice

For the salmon:

4 (3.2-ounce) portions of salmon, room temperature
Kosher salt
Extra-virgin olive oil
1 teaspoon sea salt, to finish salmon
12 cucumber flowers to garnish

To make the ragout: Sauté mushrooms in 1 teaspoon butter with shallots and salt. When fully cooked, add zucchini and remaining butter. Finish with zucchini blossoms and chives. Spoon ragout onto paper towel; keep warm and reserve.

Lightly salt foie gras and poach in olive oil at 135°F for 20 minutes. Remove from oil and chill completely.

In a small saucepan over high heat, reduce carrot juice by three-quarters; keep warm. Blend foie gras into reduced carrot juice. Add lemon juice and salt to taste.

Lightly salt salmon and poach in olive oil at 135°F for 8 minutes. Remove from oil and pat dry on paper towel. Sprinkle cooked salmon with sea salt.

To compose: Froth carrot sauce with a hand blender and add 2 tablespoons each to the bottom of 4 bowls. Divide the ragout between the bowls. Place the salmon on top of ragout and finish with cucumber flowers sprinkled on top.

Scopa

109A Plaza Street
Healdsburg, CA 95448
(707) 433-5282
www.scopahealdsburg.com
Chefs/Owners: Ari Rosen and Dawnelise Regnery Rosen

For a young, twenty-first-century chef, Ari Rosen looks the part: sculpted facial hair, sparkling eyes, and typically sporting a T-shirt instead of a chef's coat. But somehow his utter earnestness, reverence for history, and passion for what he does feel atypical. And they are key ingredients in the incredible success of his first restaurant, Scopa.

Rosen's path to chefdom and restaurant ownership is also not of the normal variety. Though he grew up in Mendocino County often mushrooming with his father and enjoying the family's prolific vegetable garden, he didn't plan to work in food. As a psychology major at Brown, he conducted brain research through sleep studies and toyed with what he wanted to do in life. Joking with one of his professors, he said maybe he'd move back to Northern California's wine country and open a wine-focused sleep lab there.

Little did he know, he was much closer to that future reality than he imagined.

After a long-distance relationship temporarily ended in heartbreak (the couple later reunited, married, and recently had their first child), Rosen moved to Italy, the land of many of his relatives, and began to cook. This was his version of culinary school, learning technique from Lorenzo Torrini, who he describes as "young, creative, amazing, and totally insane." When he began working from 8 a.m. till midnight six days a week, "it was like gasoline on fire," Rosen explains. "I knew immediately this is what I want to do." After a year with Torrini, Rosen went on to work for Luca Pecorini, who he credits with teaching him about how land, history, and ingredients tie together.

At Scopa, Rosen is most passionate about what he calls "lost ingredients"—such as an Italian varietal squash he refers to as "sweet meat," perfect for his ravioli in midwinter, and the mildly bitter Italian chicory, punterelle, that a local contract farmer grows just for him—as well as grandmothers' recipes, and not just his own. His menu has honored two separate versions of *sugo calabrese*—a traditional Calabrian sauce based on pork neck, tomatoes, and spices—from friends' grandmothers, and he still gets emotional when he remembers the families' reactions to his preparation of the dish. Another perennial menu favorite, Nonna's Tomato-Braised Chicken with an out-of-this-world creamy polenta, served stew-like and still bubbling in a miniature cast-iron pot, is a tribute to both his own grandmother and to all the diminutive, deceptively strong women he saw in Italy who would stir the polenta with their giant, name-emblazoned paddles while standing on stepstools over huge hammered-copper cauldrons.

Booked weeks in advance, the restaurant itself is tiny and shoebox-shaped, feeling simultaneously New York in its urban hipness and full of Italian tradition in its dishes—and Rosen's heart comes through in each one. Of Serafina, his young "fiery angel" daughter, the proprietor wants her to "follow her heart" in life. If she's anything like her father, her loves may converge in the kitchen.

Spicy Italian Sausage

(SERVES 4–8)

4 teaspoons kosher salt
¾ teaspoon finely ground black pepper
1 teaspoon red chili flakes (peperoncino), add ½ teaspoon more for super hot
2 teaspoons finely ground fennel seeds (use a mortar and pestle, or process in a spice grinder—a coffee bean grinder works perfectly for this task)
¾ teaspoon whole fennel seeds
1¾ teaspoons sugar
3 pounds ground pork shoulder (also called pork butt)
1¾ teaspoons garlic paste (about 2–3 garlic cloves mortar-and-pestled into a smooth paste)
3 tablespoons red wine

Mix all the dry ingredients in a small bowl.

Place the ground pork in a large mixing bowl and spread the garlic paste and wine evenly over the top of the pork. Add all the dry ingredients to the mixing bowl, sprinkling evenly throughout the pork.

Using your hands, knead the pork over and over (mix for about 10 minutes total). Every once in a while, fold the four corners of the pork back into the middle and continue kneading. You will want to keep mixing the pork until the fat begins to bind with the meat, giving it a tacky feeling that is difficult to remove from your hands. You cannot overmix.

Now your sausage is ready for use. It will last about a week tightly wrapped and refrigerated. You can break some into a pan and fry it up with peppers, use it in pastas, or put it around skewers to grill it. If you are more ambitious, you can buy casings from your local butcher and stuff the sausage into the casings. Either way, you have successfully made your first Italian sausage.

Grilled Ricotta Crostini with Roasted Eggplant & Oven-Roasted Cherry Tomatoes

(SERVES 4–6)

The ricotta and grilled bread pair together beautifully and call to mind the pastoral snack that shepherds have enjoyed for centuries. The roasted eggplant and oven-roasted cherry tomatoes make this dish sing of the fruits of late summer.

1 pint basket red cherry tomatoes
Salt
Extra-virgin olive oil
1 pound Italian long or Japanese long eggplant (there are typically about two Japanese eggplants per pound, depending on size)
15 small to medium basil leaves
1 teaspoon chili flakes
2 garlic cloves, thinly sliced
4–6 slices Italian country bread, cut 1 inch thick
Tutto Calabria hot spread, or any Italian hot chili spread (optional)
¼ pound baby arugula
2 cups (16 ounces) ricotta cheese (Bellwether preferred)

This is a simple dish that requires a fair amount of work to be done ahead of time. You will want to start the oven-roasted cherry tomatoes the day before or earlier in the morning. Cut the tomatoes in half and place them with the cut side facing up on a parchment-paper-lined baking sheet. Sprinkle salt over the tomatoes, lightly covering the tops of each. Let them sit out at room temperature for 4–24 hours, depending on how much time you have.

Preheat oven to 250°F.

Place the tray of tomatoes in the preheated oven for 45–60 minutes. If you have a convection oven, turn on the fan. You need to check them every 20 minutes since everyone's oven operates differently. Pull the tomatoes from the oven when they have reduced their size by one-third. They should look wrinkly and be the texture of delicate fruit leather. They should not turn brown or become crispy, as this would mean you cooked them too long. After pulling them from the oven, let the tomatoes cool, then toss gently in olive oil and set aside.

Preheat oven to 500°F, using the fan if you have a convection oven.

For the roasted eggplant, begin by trimming the tops and bottoms off the eggplants. These eggplants should be long and skinny (more banana shaped than softball). Cut the eggplant in half lengthwise twice, giving 4 narrow quarters. Then cut each quarter of the eggplant evenly into as many 3- to 4-inch sections as possible. You should end up with about 8 pieces per eggplant, each piece with one side that has skin. Repeat cutting with each eggplant.

Dip each piece of eggplant in olive oil, completely submerging it, and place on a parchment-paper-lined baking sheet with the skin side down. Spread out all of the eggplant so the pieces are not touching. Roast in the preheated oven for 9–15 minutes, until the eggplant turns a golden brown and is soft to the touch. Remove from oven and let cool. Once cool, toss with olive oil, whole basil leaves, chili flakes, a pinch of salt, and the thinly sliced garlic. Set aside.

This dish is best served while the bread is still warm. Grill the bread right before you plan to serve the crostini. After grilling the bread, drizzle the top with olive oil, then lightly spread with Italian hot chili (optional) and place a small handful of arugula on top, followed by the ricotta cheese (I like to spread it on about ½ inch thick). Top the ricotta with a sprinkle of salt, followed by 4–6 pieces of roasted eggplant and 4–6 cherry tomato halves. Cut the bread slices in half and serve on top of a bed of arugula, drizzling each finished crostini with olive oil.

ZAZU ON THE RIVER

52 Front Street (at Davis Family Vineyards)
Healdsburg, CA 95448
(707) 433-3858
www.zazurestaurant.com
Chefs/Owners: Duskie Estes and John Stewart

The outgrowth of a couple's passion for the farm and the pigs who roam there, zazu on the river is the newest restaurant by dynamic husband-and-wife team John Stewart and Duskie Estes. The sandwich and small plates shop—also known casually as "the Pork Shack"—follows in the footsteps of Bovolo, the couple's former popular, casual spot on the Healdsburg square.

Located at a family winery, the new restaurant–shack relies on its own huge garden and features a spacious, shaded deck—the ideal spot to enjoy a delicious wine country morsel. "We needed to get some dirt under our fingers and some room to move around in," explained John Stewart of the couple's closure and transition of Bovolo.

Though not looking to grow a restaurant empire, they started Bovolo, now zazu on the river, because they wanted a place to complement their original endeavor—zazu restaurant + farm, in Santa Rosa (featured on page 200)—in both style and, frankly, schedule. "We have kids, and needed one restaurant to be daytime-focused and the other to be at night," Estes explains. Also, they wanted an outlet for Stewart's passion: salumi.

Estes and Stewart met in Seattle nearly two decades ago, where master salumist Armandino Batali (father of Mario) wowed them with his craft. Stewart's love of pork and all manner of meats actually converted Estes (she was a vegetarian for more than twenty years beforehand). Now, not only do they both appreciate the animal and products that come from it, but they reign when it comes to pig: The couple was named "King and Queen of Pork 2011" at Grand Cochon (a culinary competition promoting heritage-breed pigs) at the Food & Wine Classic in Aspen, Colorado. They also produce their own line of bacon and sausage—Black Pig—that is exclusively offered at some of the best restaurants in the country, including Thomas Keller's The French Laundry in nearby Yountville.

The charming and wildly talented couple say they are "pioneering the new 'Slow Food . . . Fast' concept," an apt description for the new iteration of the small plates shop. Handcrafted salumi—which Stewart makes from pasture-raised heritage hogs—are featured prominently in sandwiches, pastas, and even salads. And they plan to feature a "you-pick" BLT when the new farm's fifty-five varieties of tomatoes are ripe and ready—an irresistible offering for the lover of garden-fresh ingredients.

For a quick, honest bite after a day of wine tasting in Healdsburg, zazu on the river is the perfect stop. And if you happen to see Stewart, check out his tattoo. The evidence of his pig love is clear.

ZAZU ON THE RIVER
Pickled Grapes

(SERVES 4–6)

The fat and salt of John's house-made salumi loves pickles. We serve our salumi along with these grapes (pictured in background), as we live in grape country. These are also great on chicken or pork as an entree.

1½ cups apple cider vinegar
1 cup brown sugar
1 cup water
8 ginger coins (fresh ginger cut into circles)
6 cloves
2 jalapeños, sliced into rings
2 tablespoons coriander seeds
2 cinnamon sticks
3 star anise
1 bay leaf
1 pound grapes, picked

In a nonreactive pot, combine the vinegar, sugar, water, and spices. Bring to a boil. Pour hot liquid over the grapes. Let steep at least 30 minutes.

Breakfast · Espress
Please wait to be seated...
CALISTOGA

CALISTOGA

SOUPS & SIGNATURES

Known for its famous mud baths, natural hot springs, and Old Faithful geyser, Calistoga is easily described as a funky town, stuck in a bygone era. The casual visitor feels as though he or she has been dropped into the Wild West, with the town's plentiful original signage and covered sidewalks and a true western sensibility that seems to permeate the area.

Discovered in the mid-1800s, Calistoga was originally designed as a resort town. Gold-rusher Samuel Brannan arrived determined to build the "Saratoga of California" to rival New York's Saratoga Springs as an elite spot for rejuvenation. Still drawing countless visitors daily, those hot springs are the heart of this very hot town, one of the hottest in the region, with its scrub oak–dotted ridgelines that give a sense of laid-back, authentic country living. The heat shapes the wine that comes from this area as well—its intensity is superb for growing big red wine varietals, such as the famed cabernet sauvignon of Chateau Montelena.

In some ways Calistoga still feels like a relic of the past, a spot that breaks the mold of the "quintessential wine country experience," but its restaurants are a vibrant blend of old and new—and all culinary gems of distinct varieties. From the bistro that did farm-to-table cooking "before it was cool" to a husband-wife, chef–pastry chef team that is now taking the town by storm with their modern interpretations of seasonal cuisine, Calistoga offers a surprising range of culinary experiences.

Its cuisine is simple and approachable, with a spirit that matches the relaxed vibe of the town. As part of a stroll down the main drag of Lincoln Avenue, past antiques stores, bric-a-brac shops, and countless places to rejuvenate mind, body, and soul, you can plot out each meal of the day. Though this chapter is focused primarily on soups and sides, don't be mistaken: Calistoga's restaurants provide a wealth of dining experiences. Whether it be breakfast at the famed Cafe Sarafornia or a comforting Italian lunch at Boskos Trattoria or dinner at elegant newbie JoLe, you will find a perfect setup before relaxing into a rejuvenating treatment—a luxurious cabernet wrap or lavender-infused mud bath, perhaps?—or strolling through the Petrified Forest just up the road.

All Seasons

1400 Lincoln Avenue
Calistoga, CA 94515
(707) 942-9111
www.allseasonsnapavalley.net
Owners: Gayle Keller and Alex Dierkhising
Chef: Summer Sebastiani

Outside, it looks like a simple cafe. Inside, All Seasons has the physical quality of an airy French bistro in wine country. It's a lovely, casual space, lined with a bar at the back, a collection of small tables throughout, and a workhorse of a kitchen—commanded by chef Summer Sebastiani.

Sebastiani grew up on a ranch in Sonoma County, where her parents, who she describes as "hippies," raised beef, pork, chickens, and turkeys, and a variety of vegetables in their acre-garden. Her dad was a hunter, and at home they ate duck and dove, along with freshly caught salmon, crab, and trout. "We didn't know any different." It makes sense that she is inspired by seasonal ingredients and ended up—after culinary school and working in other restaurants—at a place called All Seasons.

Owners Gayle Keller and Alex Dierkhising (brother of Drake Dierkhising of Cafe Sarafornia, page 54) opened their first restaurant more than thirty years ago, when Calistoga was an even sleepier town. The husband-and-wife team is part of a restaurant family, like others in this book, and reminisce about how they did "farm-to-table" at All Seasons, their second restaurant, before it was cool. They are passionate about fine wines, too, with accolades to prove it: Their early restaurant, Silverado, was among the first in the United States to receive the coveted Wine Spectator Grand Award for excellence in 1982.

The wine is still important in the All Seasons picture—the bistro's wine list is impressive for such a small, unassuming spot—and its wines pair well with the restaurant's eclectic "new American inspired" seasonal, of course, menu. Lobster bisque is a hugely popular menu item, so popular that it remains on the menu throughout the seasons, but the variety of sandwiches, salads, pastas, and mains all feature the loveliest of farm-fresh ingredients—oftentimes from Forni-Brown-Welsh (page 60), a local small farm that Sebastiani swears by.

The culinary team was kind enough to share both the lobster bisque recipe as well as their award-winning asparagus soup, which they advise, naturally, should be prepared at the height of asparagus season.

Lobster Bisque

(SERVES 6–8)

For the lobster stock:

3 pounds lobster bodies (you can ask your fishmonger for spent lobster carcasses or use the empty bodies after you've prepared lobster for another meal)
1 yellow or white onion, chopped
1 carrot, peeled and chopped
1 cup chopped celery
1 small bunch parsley
10 black peppercorns
3 garlic cloves

For the bisque:

½ cup butter
¼ cup all-purpose flour
2 quarts (8 cups) lobster stock
1 quart (4 cups) heavy whipping cream
1 pound Roma tomatoes, diced
1 bunch tarragon
¼ cup brandy
½ whole lemon
1 tablespoon tomato paste
Dash of cayenne pepper
Salt and pepper to taste

Preheat oven to 450°F.

Clean lobster bodies by scooping out all guts and running cold water over the bodies. Place the clean carcasses on a sheet pan and roast in a very hot oven for about 15 minutes. Place roasted carcasses in a 2-gallon stockpot, fill with water to cover, and add the remaining ingredients. Bring to a boil and hold at a simmer for 1 hour. Strain, chill, and set aside.

To make the bisque, melt the butter in a large stockpot and then add flour, stirring together to form a paste (the basis of a roux). Cook, stirring constantly with a wooden spoon, until the mixture is light brown. At that point, add the lobster stock and cream.

In a small saucepan, add tomatoes, tarragon, and brandy; sauté briefly to burn off the liquor. Add this tomato mixture to the cream-stock mixture and bring to a boil. After it reaches a boil, add the lemon half and tomato paste, reduce the heat, and simmer for 30 minutes, stirring continuously to prevent sticking. Add cayenne and salt and pepper to taste.

Remove the pot from the heat and remove the lemon from the mixture; discard lemon. Carefully ladle the mixture in small batches into a blender, blending a small amount at a time to puree (proceed with caution, as hot liquids expand exponentially upon blending—be careful not to overfill). Pass the resulting puree through a fine-mesh strainer to remove any remaining lumps. Season to taste and serve.

Asparagus Soup with Mustard Greens & Cheddar-Mustard Seed Crackers

(SERVES 4–6)

The delicate baby spinach doesn't really alter the soup's flavor, but the fresh, brilliant green color it provides is worth the addition.

For the soup:

Butter
2 large bunches mustard greens, washed and roughly chopped (center stem cut away from the leaves and discarded)
1 shallot, peeled and sliced
2 quarts (8 cups) heavy cream
1 medium yellow onion, peeled and sliced
1 garlic clove
2 large bunches asparagus, preferably pencil thin
6–7 ounces (6 cups firmly packed) baby spinach, thoroughly washed
1 tablespoon fresh lemon juice
Salt and pepper
Sprinkle of mustard sprouts (available at natural food stores), or substitute radish sprouts (optional)

For the cheddar-mustard seed crackers:

2 cups all-purpose flour
¼ cup cornmeal
2 teaspoons salt
½ teaspoon nutmeg, freshly grated if possible
Small dash of cayenne pepper, approximately ⅛ teaspoon, or substitute a few grinds of black pepper
¼ cup cold butter, cut into small pieces
1 cup good white cheddar (such as Vermont cheddar), grated
1 cup finely grated Parmesan
½ cup half-and-half
2 tablespoons whole mustard seeds

Melt enough butter in a pan to easily coat the bottom of the pan and add the chopped mustard greens and sliced shallot. Gently sauté until the greens are completely soft and wilted. Taste the greens to ascertain how peppery and intense the flavors are, since you may decide not to use all you've cooked. Set aside.

Meanwhile, place cream, sliced onion, and garlic clove in a heavy-bottomed pot. Bring to a boil, drop temperature to a simmer, and cook until onion and garlic are very soft. Turn off burner, add asparagus, and let sit for 10 minutes or more as needed to lightly cook asparagus. Put the cream-asparagus mixture in a blender and puree, alternating with the mustard greens and fresh spinach. Before adding the last of the mustard greens, taste the mixture to see if the flavor is well pronounced. If you like the level of mustard flavor, don't add any more.

Pour the soup through a fine strainer, then add the lemon juice and salt and pepper to taste. Serve immediately, topped with a sprinkle of mustard sprouts, or cool to room temperature, cover, and refrigerate until use. This is best served within 1–2 days.

To make the crackers, briefly blend flour, cornmeal, salt, nutmeg, and cayenne together in a food processor, then sprinkle butter over the ingredients. Blend briefly, then continue pulsing just until combined and mixture has a sandy-pebbly texture. Do not overmix. Combine cheddar, Parmesan, half-and-half, and mustard

seeds in a bowl, then slowly add this to the dough, just until nicely combined. Dough should be fairly firm and easy to form into a ball. Divide the dough and shape into 2 neat, even logs. Wrap tightly in plastic wrap and chill in the refrigerator at least 3 hours.

Preheat oven to 350°F.

Slice logs into thin rounds and place on a parchment-covered baking sheet. Bake for around 10 minutes, then check for even browning and rotate the pan if necessary. Bake for approximately another 5 minutes. Let cool completely on baking sheet, then place crackers in an airtight container. If not used within a few days, you may have to "refresh" them in the oven at moderate temperature for 2–3 minutes to ensure crispness.

Barolo

1457 Lincoln Avenue
Calistoga, CA 94515
(707) 942-9900
www.barolocalistoga.com
Owners/Operators: Mark Young and Ron Goldin

Sleek red leather banquettes offer the backdrop for the classic Italian dishes for which this modern little Calistoga spot is known. Owner and general manager Mark Young spent nearly a month cooking in a Calabrian restaurant in the coastal town of Maratea, Italy, in 2002, after a personal health scare led him to reevaluate life and push himself to do something more adventurous. He spoke not a word of Italian before making the decision and gave himself a crash course in the language with an eight-part series of educational CDs before setting off for another crash course—in real Italian cooking.

"The woman who owned the restaurant made absolutely everything they served," Young recalls, and through demonstration, despite Young's limited Italian, she taught him a number of "great recipes" and techniques, including how to make gnocchi.

When Young returned to the United States, he and his partner, Ron Goldin, already owned and operated three other popular restaurants in Calistoga, but decided to open Barolo as an expression of this Italy trip—and as a tribute to many of their favorite restaurants in New York City. They wanted an intimate space with an urban feel, contemporary design elements, great cocktails and excellent local wines, and, of course, fantastic food. And they got it all.

Twists on classic cocktails—like a raspberry sidecar or a negroni with a touch of blood orange puree—headline the drink menu, along with a wine list that features mostly Napa Valley (and many Calistoga-specific) wines. Named for the bold Italian red varietal—comparable to a California cabernet sauvignon—Barolo places importance on the wine as part of the dining experience, but Young and Goldin wanted to highlight the many remarkable local wines as opposed to Italian styles.

Of course, Young also brought the recipes he learned in Italy, including a rustic eggplant torte and the fabulous gnocchi, and personally taught them, just as he was taught, to his Barolo staff. So go, try the wine and sample the gnocchi, eggplant torte, or scratch pastas, and imagine you're in a tiny coastal restaurant in Italy, but with a California–New York flair.

Barolo's Arancini

(SERVES 8–12)

1½ cups dry arborio rice
½ yellow onion, finely chopped
4 cups chicken stock (preferred) or water
1 cup finely diced prosciutto
½ cup finely chopped basil
1½ cups shredded mozzarella cheese
¼ cup finely chopped parsley
½ cup flour
2½ cups panko (Japanese bread crumbs)
3 eggs
2 tablespoons milk
6 cups cooking oil

Slow-cook the arborio with onion per package instructions. Using chicken stock is better than water for this process; it will give more flavor to the rice. Spread cooked risotto evenly on a cookie sheet and allow to cool to room temperature.

Add the prosciutto, basil, mozzarella cheese, and parsley to the risotto; fold in to combine. In a separate bowl, mix together the flour and panko and set aside. In another bowl, beat the eggs with the milk and set aside.

Portion risotto mixture with a small ice-cream scoop or tablespoon into 1½-inch-diameter balls on a cookie sheet in a single layer. Working with both hands, dip a risotto ball into the egg mixture with one hand and then place in the panko-flour mixture. Using the dry hand, coat the risotto ball with the panko mixture. Set risotto balls aside in a single layer, coating all of them before starting to fry.

Heat cooking oil in a deep cast-iron skillet or Dutch oven to a temperature of 375–400°F (at this temperature, a drop of water will "spit" when dropped into oil) and carefully add 6–8 risotto balls at a time. Cook until golden brown and set on paper towels. You can hold these on a cookie sheet in a 200°F oven until all arancini are cooked.

Serve with your favorite aioli, cocktail sauce with crème fraîche, or marinara sauce.

Paola Cavazini's Eggplant Torte

(SERVES 6 AS AN ENTREE OR 8 AS AN APPETIZER)

For the cheese and egg mixture:

4 eggs, beaten
1 cup grated Parmigiano-Reggiano cheese
2/3 cup heavy cream

For the cooked cream mixture:

1 tablespoon flour
1 cup milk, divided
¾ cup heavy cream
Salt and pepper to taste
Fresh grated nutmeg to taste

For the eggplant:

3 or 4 average-size eggplants, cut into ¼-inch-thick slices
Salt to taste
Weights (approximately 20 pounds); you may use a combination of sheet pans, weighed down with cans of soup
2 cups flour
1–2 cups good quality olive oil

To assemble the torte:

2–3 cups tomato sauce (purchased, or make your own delicious sauce: fill a cookie sheet with a single layer of halved Roma tomatoes, brush with olive oil, salt with fleur de sel, sprinkle with freshly ground pepper, and bake in a a 200°F oven for 8–10 hours; let cool and process in a food processor but don't over puree; it's very easy and absolutely worth the time)
¾–1 cup grated smoked Fontina cheese
¼ cup grated Parmigiano-Reggiano cheese

Mix together the eggs, Parmigiano-Reggiano, and heavy cream; cover and refrigerate.

To prepare the cream mixture, whisk flour and ¼ cup milk together in a small saucepan over medium heat. Using a wooden spoon, add the rest of the milk and the cream and heat over medium-high heat until the sauce bubbles gently. Keep stirring while it bubbles, 5–10 minutes, or until it is thick enough for you to see the bottom of the pan as you pull the spoon across the bottom. Remove from heat, cool the mixture down, and season with salt, pepper, and grated nutmeg.

To make the eggplant, lightly salt both sides of the eggplant slices, lay them in a single layer between towels, and weigh them down with 20 pounds of weight for at least 4 hours and up to 10 hours. After moisture has been pressed out of the eggplant, dredge the eggplant slices in flour and fry in hot olive oil (oil should be about ½-inch deep in the pan) for about 1½ minutes per side, or until lightly golden. Drain on towels to absorb excess oil.

To assemble the torte, preheat oven to 350°F. Have the cheese and egg mixture, cooked cream mixture, tomato sauce, and the two cheeses at your station and ready to go. Cover the bottom of a half hotel pan (or baking dish) with a thin layer of the cooked cream mixture. Arrange half of the eggplant slices over the cream mixture, then add a layer of Fontina cheese and tomato sauce. Spread half of the cheese-egg mixture over the tomato sauce. Lay the rest of the eggplant over the sauce, cover with Fontina cheese, cheese-egg mixture, tomato sauce, and finally the cooked cream.

Sprinkle with Parmigiano-Reggiano cheese and bake 35–40 minutes. Let the torte rest at least 30 minutes before cutting, and dress the plate with any leftover tomato sauce.

B CELLARS

400 Silverado Trail, Calistoga, CA 94515
(877) 229-9939 · www.bcellars.com
Cofounder and Principal: Jim Borsack
Master Winemaker: Kurt Venge; Chef: Christina Machamer

A food-centric winery and tasting room with an expanding culinary program would naturally look to a Gordon Ramsay–endorsed chef to run its food program, right? Maybe it's not an expected fit, but it is a superb one in the case of B Cellars and talented young chef Christina Machamer.

St. Louis native Machamer won the fourth season of Ramsay's popular network TV cooking competition, *Hell's Kitchen,* and after going on to help Ramsay open his eponymous restaurant at The London West Hollywood hotel—quickly earning a Michelin star—she went on to other endeavors, including at Thomas Keller's Bouchon bistro in Beverly Hills.

Machamer has studied at The Culinary Institute of America in both Hyde Park and St. Helena—the latter is where she completed a program in viticulture, becoming a certified sommelier through a rigorous exam from the Court of Master Sommeliers, based in London. Her desire to immerse herself in the wine side of things led her to B Cellars.

Being that Machamer is at the food helm of a winery that "celebrates the blending of wine from different vineyards but also from different varietals," her focus is on extracting the richness of the terroir and on capturing umami, or the savory taste, to complement the salt (Maldon sea salt at B Cellars), sour (they use lemon), sweet (figs and apples), and bitter (limes).

"We look for balance in our food and how it interacts with tannins," Machamer explains. "In the right combination, we've created the fifth taste, umami."

She works closely with winemaker Kirk Venge and does not confine herself to the kitchen—she also participates in harvest, brings in grapes, and coordinates wine dinners.

"Every decision we make at B Cellars is food-centric," says Machamer, explaining that, as a result, the team has grown together and created a food and wine program that they are all proud of.

Boskos Trattoria

1364 Lincoln Avenue
Calistoga, CA 94515
(707) 942-9088
www.boskos.com
Owner: John Seeger; Chef: Don Garrett

Fried polenta—that's where we'll start. Addictive, comforting, hearty, and delicate all at once, this popular starter is a signal of what you're in for with a meal at Boskos.

There's more to the nearly thirty-year-old trattoria than one might initially imagine while standing on the covered sidewalk outside. Chef Don Garrett is passionate and experienced, having spent time in some of the wine country's most renowned kitchens, starting with an apprenticeship at the Sonoma Mission Inn and Spa at the tender age of fifteen and working his way through the kitchens of the region over the next three decades. A Sonoma native, Garrett is a champion of California cuisine—which he describes as a blend of fresh, local, and sustainable ingredients with cutting-edge international culinary techniques—and loves teaching cooking classes and doing demonstrations aimed at helping others "unlock their inner chef."

At Boskos, Garrett enjoys honoring traditional Italian cookery—including making beautiful fresh mozzarella and burrata (a cheese made with fresh mozzarella and cream) from scratch—and the trattoria's cuisine reflects that commitment to local, fresh ingredients. The restaurant kitchen he commands sits at the back of the spacious-but-cozy dining room and is open to show off its cooks stretching pizza dough and cutting fresh pastas throughout service.

Some diners come once a week and are pleased to have their regular table. Others may stop in for lunch or dinner while passing through town, perhaps between mud bath treatments or wine tastings. All should try a fresh pasta, one of the unusually delicious sweet-sour-crusted pizzas (they use rye flour in the dough, giving it its special tangy quality), and, of course, that heady polenta. Nearly everything possible is cooked in the restaurant's wood-burning oven, and you can taste the pride in each dish. Be forewarned: The portions are more than generous. You will not leave hungry.

Boskos Minestrone

(SERVES 15; YIELDS APPROXIMATELY 1½ GALLONS OF SOUP)

½ cup oil (canola or a non-extra-virgin olive oil)
2 tablespoons chopped garlic
1 pound yellow onions, cut into ½-inch dice
1 large carrot, cut into ½-inch dice
½ bunch celery, leaves removed, stalks cut into ½-inch dice
2 leeks, white part only, cut into ½-inch dice
½ head green cabbage, chopped into ½-inch dice
2 tablespoons kosher salt
¾ teaspoon white pepper
¾ teaspoon red chili pepper flakes
¾ teaspoon paprika
1 tablespoon dried oregano
1 tablespoon dried basil
1½ cups crushed tomatoes
⅛ cup beef base
3 quarts chicken stock or water
1 cup dry (or 2 cups cooked) cannellini beans
1 teaspoon salt
1 bay leaf
1 pound red potatoes, cut into ½-inch dice
¾ pound zucchini, cut into ½-inch dice
¼ bunch (approximately 1 ½ cups) fresh Swiss chard or spinach
½ pound shell noodles, uncooked
Salt and pepper to taste

Start with a large stockpot over medium-high heat; add oil.

When the oil is hot, add the garlic. Once the garlic starts to brown slightly, add the diced onions, diced carrots, diced celery, sliced leeks, and diced cabbage; cook for about 5 minutes, still over medium-high heat. Add the salt, white pepper, pepper flakes, paprika, oregano, and basil during this first sauté process—adding dry seasonings early helps create layers of flavors in a dish. You may need to add more salt and pepper to reflect your taste. (You may sauté these items separately if you like, but be sure all the vegetables become translucent before adding the water or stock.)

Add tomatoes, beef base, and water or stock to the pot with the vegetables; bring entire mixture to a simmer.

Meanwhile, if using dry cannellini beans: Cook the cannellini beans in boiling, salted water with a bay leaf until beans are soft (approximately 20 minutes). Once beans are done (or if starting with cooked beans), set half aside. Puree the other half in a food mill, food processor, or blender. Add the whole, cooked beans and the pureed beans to the soup.

When the soup comes to a simmer, add the potatoes. Let the soup continue to boil for 5 minutes, then add the zucchini and chard to the pot. Cook mixture for another 5 minutes.

Add the shell noodles and cook for a final 5 minutes. Make sure the pasta and potatoes are cooked but not overcooked by removing and tasting for the right texture (al dente—tender, but still a bit firm). Adjust the salt and pepper to your liking.

Brannan's

1374 Lincoln Avenue
Calistoga, CA 94515
(707) 942-2233
www.brannansgrill.com
Owners/Operators: Mark Young and Ron Goldin

A classic American steak house, Brannan's was the second restaurant Mark Young and Ron Goldin opened together in Calistoga. And it is a beauty.

Hand-forged metalwork and gorgeous redwood timbers highlight this California Craftsman–style space, and Young's pride of design is clear in the way he talks about the restaurant. "Everything was made by local artisan builders," he explains, marveling at how good the space still looks after fourteen years.

Young has always had an eye for design, and he worked just about every restaurant job before meeting Goldin, who owned the town's popular family pizza and pasta joint, Checkers. A Bay Area native, Young worked for legendary female San Francisco restaurateurs in the 1960s and '70s, including Sally Stanford and Juanita Musson, as well as in food and beverage for the Marriott hotels and the elegant Westin St. Francis, finally landing at the posh Auberge du Soleil (page 138), which he still describes as "magical." There he learned about the art of the restaurant, likening it to show business. "When the doors open," Young says, "it's like the show begins."

As the story goes, in 1991, at the conclusion of an arduous hike to the top of Yosemite Falls with Goldin, Goldin convinced him to open a second Checkers. Young says he was too exhausted by the end of the hike to stand a chance against the idea. Then again, a few years later, when another space in town that had been occupied by restaurants for more than sixty years was suddenly empty, they decided to take on a new project and opened Brannan's.

And the town is still pleased they did. Young and Goldin locally source as many of their ingredients as possible, including mostly grass-fed beef from Sonoma and Marin Counties, oysters from nearby Tomales Bay, and tomatoes from their own backyard. Trellised, unusually, in rows like grapes, the tomato "vineyards" are harvested by Young and Goldin themselves, in 200-pound batches at a time.

For what may seem like a typical steak house from the outside, the personal touch and commitment to the dining experience is evident throughout the Brannan's space. Young invites all to come and enjoy the show—and to let him know how you like his tomatoes.

Brannan's Mac & Cheese Cakes

(SERVES 6–8)

1 cup butter
¼ cup flour
2 cups heavy cream
1 cup milk
4 cups grated cheddar cheese
1½ cups grated Monterey Jack cheese
2–3 teaspoons grated nutmeg to taste
1 pound dry elbow macaroni
Salt and pepper to taste
Up to 2 cups regular or panko bread crumbs

Preheat oven to 350°F.

Heat a medium saucepan over medium-high heat. Make a roux by melting the butter in the saucepan and stirring in the flour, continuing to cook and stirring constantly until the roux turns a golden color. Set aside.

In a large saucepan or stockpot, bring the cream and milk to a simmer, then add the cheeses and nutmeg.

In a separate stockpot, cook and drain the macaroni. Add the cooked macaroni to the cream-and-cheese mixture. Add salt and pepper to taste.

From here, you can place the mac and cheese in a baking dish, top with ½–1 cup bread crumbs (to your taste), and bake in the preheated oven for 30 minutes or until "set." Or, you can pour the mixture into a baking dish and, using a wooden spoon, mix in 1½–2 cups bread crumbs. Refrigerate until it is set, then spoon the mac and cheese onto a parchment-paper-lined sheet pan and lightly press into 4- to 5-inch-diameter cakes. You would then cook the cakes over medium heat in a nonstick skillet with a little olive oil, about 5 minutes per side, turning once for delicious and crusty cakes.

Brannan's Baked Marrow Bones with Parsley Salad & Salsa Verde

(SERVES 6–8)

For the salsa verde:

¼–½ cup olive oil
1 bunch Italian parsley, stemmed
4 garlic cloves
3 tablespoons capers
4–6 anchovy fillets
Salt and pepper to taste

For the marrow bones and to plate:

1 sourdough baguette
3 lemons
2–3 tablespoons olive oil
2–3 pounds beef shank bones, cut into 3- to 4-inch sections
½ cup flour
1 bunch Italian parsley, stemmed
Maldon sea salt or other high-quality sea salt to taste

To make the salsa verde, add ¼ cup olive oil and parsley to a food processor and pulse until rough chopped, not pureed. Add the garlic, capers, and anchovy and pulse until ingredients are rough chopped. Add more olive oil if necessary; the overall texture should be wet like a salsa but not overly oily. Season with salt and fresh ground pepper and set aside.

Slice the baguette into ¼-inch thickness and grill or bake until slightly toasted; set aside. Cut lemons in half and grill for 10 minutes for color and caramelization; set aside.

Preheat oven to 375°F.

Heat 2–3 tablespoons olive oil in a large skillet over medium-high heat. Dip ends of the marrow bones in flour and stand end-up in skillet; cook for approximately 2 minutes per end, turning once. Spoon a little of the salsa verde onto one end of the marrow bones and place in the oven for approximately 10–15 minutes or until a skewer inserted into marrow bone end pierces the marrow easily; remove from oven.

To assemble the dish, you can either plate each portion or place on one large platter to serve family-style, which gets everyone involved and is very impressive when served. Place the stemmed, washed, and dried parsley leaves on the plate or platter, then place the roasted marrow bones on top. Spoon the remaining salsa verde over and around the bones, wetting the parsley underneath. Place the grilled lemon halves around the edge of the plate along with the sea salt in teaspoon-size piles and 4–5 pieces of grilled baguette per person, in little stacks.

To eat, lay the bones on their sides, insert a cocktail fork or marrow knife into the bones, and pull the roasted marrow out. Place a small portion of parsley on a toast point; add little of the marrow, some salsa verde, a pinch of sea salt, and a light squeeze of lemon; and enjoy the perfect bite.

Cafe Sarafornia

1413 Lincoln Avenue
Calistoga, CA 94515
(707) 942-0555
www.cafesarafornia.com
Owners/Operators: Madeline and Drake Dierkhising

Drake and Madeline Dierkhising are the kind of people who pitch a tent in their backyard for an impromptu camping adventure with their grandchildren. They're also the sort of folks who welcome an interviewer into the very same backyard for a chat and a spot of gazpacho on a warm summer day. And, yes, they are like the types of characters who appear in the movies.

Their beloved little restaurant, Cafe Sarafornia, is in fact a movie star: It appeared in the 2008 Japanese version of the acclaimed wine-hero movie, *Sideways,* chosen for its quality as a quintessential, funky cafe in the quintessential, funky wine country town of Calistoga.

The Midwesterner, Drake, met his Boston love, Madeline, when she worked at his family's bar in Minnesota. Since marrying in 1966, they have crisscrossed the country in thirteen transcontinental moves and traveled the world, partly through Drake's former longtime job, running US Navy Officers Clubs. But it was Drake's three years in Egypt as a kid—spurred by his father's job in the Navy—that first opened his eyes to "seeing new foods," a history still apparent in the cafe's eclectic menu.

Mostly breakfast and lunch items, Cafe Sarafornia's menu includes a few of Madeline's takes on her *Sunset Magazine* favorites and classic breakfast dishes, including a beloved French toast and, according to Drake, "the best huevos rancheros you'll ever know!" A great, simple daily soup is always derived from Drake's straightforward vegetable base, "always starting with a mirepoix," and is consistently delicious.

Admitting they've had "no road map" for their path together, simply taking advantage of new opportunities as they have come about, the Dierkhisings have established a true fixture in the community with Cafe Sarafornia, not their first popular restaurant in wine country, but the current and longstanding favorite. Waitstaff is often multigenerational, with mothers and daughters working alongside each other. Local celebrities are regulars, including the late John "Doc" Wilkinson, founder of the town's famous and still thriving 1952 original hot springs resort, who used to come in so often, he had his own seat. Customers leave their mark by scrawling on a special wall at the restaurant—and show their support by photographing the cafe's bumper stickers in far-flung locations and sharing the shots with the Dierkhisings. Drake was once directed by one of his longtime servers to buy three ladies their breakfast because they'd just lost their mother, who'd been a cafe regular. "That's our staff, and our customers. We're like family."

Gazpacho Sevillano

(SERVES 4)

Sevillano means "of Seville," a major cultural and financial city in southern Spain.

- 2 small garlic cloves, peeled and crushed
- 1 small green pepper, core and seeds removed
- ½ small Spanish (yellow) onion, peeled
- 4 large ripe tomatoes (canned is okay)
- ½ cucumber, seeded
- 2–3 tablespoons vinegar (preferably sherry vinegar), depending on personal taste
- 4 cups ice water
- Salt to taste
- Olive oil to taste
- For thc *Madrilono* (or "of Madrid") version, add dry bread crumbs to taste (optional)
- Garnish with finely chopped green pepper, onion, and cucumber, or croutons (if not preparing the *Madrileno* version), to your taste (optional)

Puree and strain (or skip straining for a thick gazpacho) the first 5 ingredients, then add the vinegar, ice water, and salt to taste. Refrigerate for 1 or 2 days to meld flavors.

Add olive oil only at the time of serving, as the olive oil flavors will be fresher and not chilled. Optional: Garnish with finely chopped green pepper, onion, and cucumber, or croutons (if not preparing the *Madrileno* version), to your taste. If you choose to prepare the *Madrileno* version, add dry bread crumbs to taste before serving.

Sarafornia's Vegetable Soup

(SERVES 6)

The cabbage and tomato are the key flavor vegetables for this soup. Also, for all chopped vegetables in this recipe, a larger, rougher chop looks and works best.

- 2–3 tablespoons extra-virgin olive oil, for sautéing as needed
- 1 Spanish (yellow) onion, thinly sliced and sautéed
- 1 green pepper, chopped
- 2 large carrots, chopped
- 1 rib celery, sliced crosswise
- ½ head of cabbage, chopped
- Variety of mushrooms, parsnips, kale, or other vegetables (if you add soft vegetables, such as zucchini, add them near the end) (optional)
- 3 tomatoes, roughly chopped (or canned tomatoes)
- 1 quart (4 cups) water
- Herbs, such as parsley or bay, depending on personal taste (optional)
- Salt to taste
- Black pepper and Tabasco sauce to taste (optional)

Place a large stockpot over medium-high heat. When pot is hot, add extra-virgin olive oil. Once oil shimmers (indicating it is hot), add onion, green pepper, carrots, celery, cabbage, and any optional vegetables, and sauté until cooked to your taste. (Celery is the best gauge—when it is bite-tender, all vegetables should be done.) When onion is translucent and vegetables begin to soften, add tomatoes and water to cover, along with optional herbs; bring mixture to a boil, and then reduce to a simmer. Simmer until the vegetables are cooked but not mush—about 20 minutes.

About the salt: Adding salt is key, as is how it is added. Add salt only until you first taste the salt, and then stop.

Add water anytime you feel it needs to be added. Remember, it is meant to be a soup, not a stew.

Taste before serving; add more salt, as well as pepper and Tabasco, to your preference, as well as any additional fresh, chopped herbs (such as parsley) to garnish, if you'd like. Also, the soup is quite versatile—you may add chicken or beef, rice or noodles.

SCHRAMSBERG

1400 Schramsberg Road, Calistoga, CA 94515
(707) 942-4558 · www.schramsberg.com
President/Chief Executive Officer/Winemaker: Hugh Davies

Schramsberg is a winery of stunning beauty located in the hills above Calistoga on a 220-acre estate—and it has a long, elegant, and historic legacy. It was the second winery (Charles Krug was the first) to be built in the Napa Valley, in 1862 by Jacob Schram. Its original wine cave was built with picks and shovels, and by the end of the century, it was the largest in the valley. And Robert Louis Stevenson's *The Silverado Squatters,* which mentioned Schram's wines, helped put the winery on the map. Since then the winery has continued to grow and gain renown. Its land now totals 35,000 square feet, and the winery was declared an official historic landmark in 1957.

Hugh Davies, president, chief executive officer, and winemaker, was born in 1965, the same year his family purchased the Schramsberg property. His parents, Jack and Jamie Davies, were novices to the winemaking business when they bought the property, but were the first to use premium chardonnay and pinot noir grapes. They wanted to create the first world-class sparkling wine in the traditional *methode champenoise* style—which involves a secondary fermentation in the bottle—and they have succeeded.

Hugh studied enology at the University of California at Davis; interned at Möet et Chandon in Epernay, studying champagne production; worked for Remy Martin in the Cognac region of France; and gradually made his way back to the family business. Of his successful career in winemaking, he admits, "This was all available to me because of the hard work of my parents. As my father used to say, owning and operating a successful winery is a long-term proposition."

On average it takes three to five years for Schramsberg to produce its exceptional bottle-fermented sparkling wine, and Hugh says that what determines a great wine is the quality of the grape when picked. Schramsberg harvests when its grapes are between 17 and 23 Brix (a measurement of the level of sugars in the fruit). The team also uses the rarely seen Flora grape in the Schramsberg Crémant Demi-sec, an off-dry wine and a perfect pairing for desserts.

The winemakers look for crisp, vibrant characteristics in their grapes, with well-balanced acidity. The Carneros appellation is the best, Davies explains, as San Francisco Bay's location along the appellation's southern border creates a microclimate perfect for producing chardonnay. Davies believes his family is doing what the Schrams would have wanted. The James Beard Foundation would likely agree. In 1996 the foundation awarded Schramsberg the Wine and Spirits Professional Award for "making a significant impact in the wine and spirits industry."

JoLe

1457 Lincoln Avenue
Calistoga, CA 94515
(707) 942-5938
www.jolerestaurant.com
Chefs/Owners: Matt and Sonjia Spector

Though they met and ran their own restaurant in Philadelphia, Matt and Sonjia Spector were actually married in California's wine country, and they returned in 2008 to open their charming, simple bistro that perfectly represents the bounty of the region, JoLe.

The contemporary American restaurant sits in the historic Mount View Hotel, in a space that was once home to acclaimed chef Jan Birnbaum's Catahoula restaurant. The Spectors are intent on honoring this important culinary legacy, and are doing a beautiful job of it each night.

With simple decor, natural wood surfaces, and a huge wood-fired brick oven, the restaurant is a perfect venue for capturing what the Spectors call "the casual wine country pace." The team offers tasteful presentations of game, fowl, and fresh local fish each night and has a commitment to organic products. They share a deep appreciation for local farmers, who are clearly a critical part of their cuisine. "We wanted closer access to the farmers," they explain, given that both the chefs and their diners appreciate the role of the farmer in JoLe's dishes.

Matt, who grew up in South Jersey, is a self-proclaimed "bourbon and beer" kind of guy and got his start in the kitchen early: As a kid, he worked behind the deli counter in his uncle's butcher shop, which eventually grew into a full-scale restaurant. Always self-taught, Matt gradually began a career that led him to Philadelphia, where he worked with Susanna Foo and at Brassiere Perrier before opening his own successful restaurant, Matyson—where he met his future wife, business partner, and pastry chef, Sonjia. Because they married here, they always wanted to return to the Napa Valley to open a restaurant, and did so five years later.

Sonjia was inspired by the desserts and pastries her mother and grandmother prepared when she was a child, and she continues to create updated versions of these traditional, delicious sweets. The couple's cooking at JoLe is modern yet simple, in a style they call "New American"—designed around refined, sensible flavor profiles that resonate with their guests.

At the dinner-only JoLe, the team offers nightly four-, five-, or six-course tasting menus, along with more than fifty-five wines by the glass, including domestic, old world, and new world selections, and a small bar featuring handcrafted cocktails and spirited infusions. The Spectors enjoy their relationships with many young winemakers, who often frequent the restaurant "and share their wines with us." The couple is thrilled with the wine country experience—to be part of the group of artisans and craftsmen who are also inspired by the region's rich terroir, amazing climate, and spectacular vineyards—and we are delighted that they are here.

Tomato Shellfish Bisque

(SERVES 8)

3 lobster bodies, chopped
1 quart (4 cups) shrimp shells
1 Dungeness crab carcass, top removed and chopped
2 ounces extra-virgin olive oil
1 quart (4 cups) peeled plum tomatoes
6 garlic cloves, chopped
1 yellow onion, chopped (medium dice)
1 thumb ginger, peeled and chopped
2 carrots, chopped (medium dice)
1 jalapeño, chopped
2 cups dry vermouth (use just shy of 2 cups for the bisque; set the rest aside for a martini)
1 cup white rice
1 quart (4 cups) heavy cream
Salt to taste
1 pound crabmeat for garnish
Optional: lemon juice, lime juice, or sherry vinegar to taste

In a heavy pot, sauté lobster, shrimp, and crab bodies in olive oil. Once fragrant, add vegetables and sauté about 5 more minutes, moving ingredients around with a wooden spoon. Deglaze with vermouth and cook until almost dry.

Add rice and about 3 quarts of water to the pot. Bring to a boil, then simmer about 20–25 minutes. Add cream and bring back to a boil. Pull from the heat and let rest for 5 minutes. Puree all ingredients (except crabmeat) in a blender; strain pureed mixture through a chinoise or fine-mesh strainer.

Reheat bisque, season with salt to taste and serve with lump crabmeat as garnish.

A little acid to finish is a good idea—lemon, lime, or sherry vinegar works well.

FORNI-BROWN-WELSH FARMS

1214 Pine Street at Cedar Street, Calistoga, CA 94515
(707) 942-6123
Farmers/Owners: Lynn Brown, Peter Forni, and Barney Welsh

Walking the garden with master gardener, innovator, and visionary Lynn Brown is truly inspiring. What began in 1979 as the realization of a dream to create a fully organic and unique farm experience has become the favorite farm of renowned chefs throughout the Napa and Sonoma Valleys and across the entire Bay Area, and it feels like a rare, special opportunity to be able to see the impressive and inspired operation in person.

Brown started this farm, which borders the Napa River, with Peter Forni and Barney Welsh. The group provides Napa Valley chefs with amazing produce, including peppers, lettuces, culinary herbs, and heirloom tomatoes of the most pristine quality. Originally growing for a co-op in wine country, Brown's first customer, in 1981, was the then chef at Auberge du Soleil (page 138), Masataka Kobayashi, who later went on to open his eponymous San Francisco restaurant, Masa's, to much acclaim. But when Kobayashi approached Brown, he wanted one hundred pounds of elephant garlic. Though the request was well beyond the farm's capacity, it was then that Brown realized that he could make a living at being a farmer.

Brown joined forces with Forni, who had been managing a local vineyard, and Welsh, a property owner in Calistoga who was inspired by the endeavor, and Forni-Brown-Welsh was born. The venerated local farm grows a variety of lettuces—prized by chefs throughout the valley, some of them Michelin-starred—using what Brown refers to as "floating row covers," his secret to producing vibrant baby greens. These thin fabrics function as greenhouses, letting sunlight and water in while protecting the delicate crops. Forni-Brown-Welsh was also the first farm in the Napa wine country to grow arugula and purslane, now coveted by many chefs. The farm's pristine mixed baby gem lettuces are so freshly picked, they arrive at local restaurants still glistening with the morning dew.

The farm also produces seventy varieties of tomatoes. Famous food writer Mimi Sheraton actually put the farm's Giant Syrian heirloom tomato on the map when she visited the region and, not an heirloom tomato fan, fell in love with the varietal. The farm grows an array of edible herbs, olives, and black walnuts, and even offers purple and white garlic flowers—a best seller—which Brown recommends tossed in a salad to give a light, fragrant garlic essence against a vinaigrette.

Peppers are an important part of the Forni-Brown-Welsh product profile—many are mild and sweet, while a few are incredibly spicy. When preparing peppers to be harvested for seed, Brown advises home gardeners to overripen the fruits on the plant, letting them grow until they are wilted to ensure the seeds are viable. Fillet the flesh first, he says, and then remove and dry the seeds, preferably in natural sunlight to further foster viability.

One of the most interesting crops is the farm's collection of elusive ghost peppers. Originally from the Assam region of northeastern India, these ultrahot peppers measure more than one million units on the Scoville scale, a standard for determining heat strength in pepper types. In comparison, the jalapeño ranks 800, and the habanero, commonly believed to be one of the hottest peppers on the market, reaches only 300,000 Scoville units. Brown makes a special powder from the ghost peppers to help protect the farm's organic offerings from rabbits and other creatures who have a particular fondness for the little gem lettuce.

Those in the know can take advantage of the farm's annual public spring plant sale—every Thursday through Sunday in April and Thursday through Saturday in May. Local chefs anticipate this extremely popular event that has become a "must do" in the wine country. The sale offers a chance to snag plants and herb starts specially produced on the farm, such as baby lettuces, squashes, numerous varieties of cucumbers, culinary herbs, and an extensive array of pepper varietals, including passilla, serrano, cayenne, scotch bonnet, fatalii, bishop's cap, and Brazilian pickling peppers. Patrons also have access to a selection of heirloom seeds, all produced and propagated on the farm.

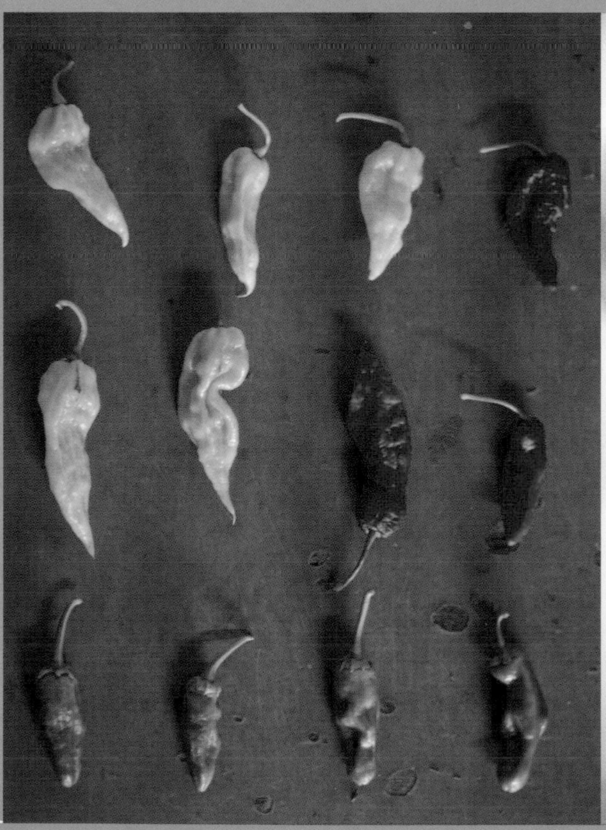

SONOMA

SALADS & SMALL PLATES

Sonoma—or "Slow-noma," as many locals affectionately call it—is a simultaneously sleepy but vibrant town "on the other side" of wine country. Commonly compared to Napa, Sonoma is almost like its laid-back sibling, organized around a classically picturesque town square, replete with a historic California mission anchoring one corner and original city hall in the center.

Situated between the Mayacamas Mountains and the Pacific Ocean, Sonoma lies on the southern border of its county. Its first inhabitants, the Wappo Native American tribe, were known for exceptional basket weaving. Today, traditions of artistry continue in winemaking and the culinary realm; the region's viticultural diversity makes it a standout in wine country. Marked by cool breezes blowing up from San Francisco Bay as well as the natural warmth of the valley itself, the eighteen-mile stretch is also perfumed by eucalyptus, abundant in the area. First dubbed "the Valley of the Moon" (the meaning of the word *Sonoma*) the quaint winemaking town still evokes a simple sort of romance more than two hundred years later.

Sonomans are full of pride in their little town and the food that comes from it, with its Italian roots and completely cosmopolitan modern-day collection of restaurants. The town truly feels lived in, and its residents frequently descend upon the square to celebrate a variety of festivals throughout the year. Author Jack London and wine visionaries Ernest and Julio Gallo are among Sonoma's more famous previous residents, making for a remarkable blend of the past and present that makes the place so unique. Agriculture is the backbone of the community here, and there is a countrified quality that permeates this modern little spot in wine country—it's an experience not to be missed.

Cafe La Haye

140 East Napa Street
Sonoma, CA 95476
(707) 935-5994
www.cafelahaye.com
Owner: Saul Gropman; Chef: Jeffrey Lloyd

Cafe La Haye is the quintessential neighborhood joint, but of the quite sophisticated variety. The restaurant is named for the former steel foundry in which it is housed, and it still has relics from the building's original use and modern tributes to its history—like the intricate ironwork that serves as a gate between the dining room and kitchen.

Proprietor Saul Gropman, a classical guitarist and former college music teacher by training and now twenty-year restaurateur by happenstance, greets you warmly as you walk in.

"I've always loved food—even as a twenty-one-year-old master's candidate in music," Gropman shares. "I love the whole orchestration of the restaurant," a sentiment that rings true when you watch him almost conducting the evening's movements around the small space. With a partly elevated dining area and teensy open kitchen, the diner has a fantastic view of everything, including chef Jeffrey Lloyd's artistic, classics-inspired creations being shuttled quickly to each table.

After working for acclaimed San Francisco restaurateur and chef Michael Mina for a number of years, Lloyd is pleased to be operating on a smaller scale at Cafe La Haye. He aptly describes Sonoma as "a small town but with a big intellect" and says he was pleasantly surprised when the street cleaner waved at him and his daughter on their first day in town.

His food, though, doesn't feel limited by a small-town sensibility. Lloyd derives inspiration from the seasons, local products, and the classics. He wants the diner to leave saying, "Wow, that was just great—and very simple." A delightfully charred prawn starter—skewered on a sprig of rosemary and nestled in a pillow of olive-studded polenta—is one of those simple, wow-inducing dishes, along with a beautiful, moist quail entree and out-of-this-world butterscotch pudding to finish.

Lloyd's cuisine is a perfect match for Gropman's own food heritage. His childhood palate was shaped by his homemaker mother's "very adventurous" tendencies in a 1960s kitchen. "She loved sauces, richness, and complexity," he shares, confiding that, as with music, he also likes foods that "bring back feelings."

Bustling, convivial, elegant, and homey all at once, Cafe La Haye will quickly become one of those restaurants where you imagine yourself a weekly regular. Chances are, Gropman will remember your favorite table.

Salad of Grilled Peach & Chilled Swiss Chard, Topped with Fresh Burrata

(SERVES 4)

10 cups Swiss chard (preferably organic), stems removed and leaves chopped
6 shallots, peeled and sliced
2 tablespoons extra-virgin olive oil
Salt and pepper to taste
Agrumato (lemon extra-virgin olive oil), as needed
2/3 cup pine nuts, toasted
¼ cup golden raisins, reconstituted in water
2 ripe peaches (Frog Hollow preferred)
2 (4-ounce) balls of fresh burrata
Pinch of Maldon sea salt
Aged balsamico, as needed

In a medium sauté pan over medium-high heat, lightly wilt Swiss chard with shallots in olive oil; add salt and pepper and chill. Mix in 2 tablespoons Agrumato, pine nuts, and raisins.

Cut peaches into quarters. Remove pits, brush with olive oil, and sprinkle with salt and pepper. In a hot grill pan or on a grill, grill until tender and lightly caramelized.

Cut burrata balls in half. Drizzle with Agrumato and sprinkle with Maldon sea salt.

Arrange salad to your preference on the plate. Finish with a drizzle of aged balsamico.

Rosemary Grilled Prawn Salad with Pepperonata & Black Olive–Parmesan Dressing

(SERVES 4)

For the prawns and to plate:

12 pieces 16/20 count shrimp, peeled and deveined
4 rosemary sprigs, long and stiff, plus 1 tablespoon chopped rosemary (removed from stems)
4 garlic cloves, finely chopped
½ cup extra-virgin olive oil
2 heirloom tomatoes, sliced
Salt and pepper to taste
6 cups arugula, cleaned
¼ cup black olive–Parmesan dressing
1 baguette, sliced and toasted
¼ cup pepperonata
4–5 tablespoons chopped herbs, to taste

For the chopped herbs (to be used in pepperonata and finished dish):

4 sprigs parsley, finely chopped
4 chives, finely chopped
4 stems thyme, woody stems removed and leaves finely chopped

For the pepperonata:

6 tablespoons tomato paste
½ cup vegetable stock
1 teaspoon Piment d'Espelette (a French red chili pepper powder), or substitute your favorite ground chili pepper
1 tablespoon chopped herbs
6 sweet red peppers, roasted, peeled, seeded, and sliced
½ cup piquillo peppers (these are fire-roasted and canned in Spain, then shipped to the United States), cut in half lengthwise and then again crosswise
Salt and pepper to taste
1 tablespoon extra-virgin olive oil
1 teaspoon lemon juice

For the black olive–Parmesan dressing:

1 whole egg
1 egg yolk
1 tablespoon lemon juice
1 tablespoon Dijon mustard
1 tablespoon chopped garlic
½ cup niçoise olives (pitted)
2 anchovy fillets
1 teaspoon Worcestershire sauce
3½ cups pure olive oil (or canola oil)
½ cup grated Parmesan cheese
Salt and pepper to taste

To prepare the prawns, skewer shrimp onto rosemary sprigs, 3 on each sprig. Marinate in chopped rosemary and garlic with ¼ cup extra-virgin olive oil; set aside for 2–4 hours. When ready to serve, grill shrimp (on the rosemary skewers) in a grill pan over high heat (or on a grill) until shrimp turns pink, indicating doneness.

To make the pepperonata, caramelize tomato paste on low heat in sauté pan for 5 minutes. Add vegetable stock, chili pepper, and chopped herbs and mix with sliced roasted peppers. Season with salt and pepper to taste, then add extra-virgin olive oil and lemon juice.

To make the dressing, add eggs, lemon juice, mustard, garlic, olives, anchovy, and Worcestershire sauce to a food processor. Turn on high speed and drizzle in oil very slowly until emulsion is set. Add remaining oil. Finish with Parmesan cheese and salt and pepper to taste. (Reserve extra dressing for use up to 1 week.)

To assemble the dish, arrange tomatoes on a plate. Season with salt and pepper and drizzle with extra-virgin olive oil. Toss arugula with extra-virgin olive oil and salt to taste. Artistically smear a tablespoon of dressing on the plate. Place a piece of toasted baguette (crostini) on top of dressing. Top crostini with pepperonata, set grilled shrimp on top of pepperonata, top with bit of dressed arugula, sprinkle entire dish with chopped herbs as desired, and enjoy.

Depot Hotel Restaurant and Garden

241 First Street West
Sonoma, CA 95476
(707) 938-2980
www.depotsonoma.com
Owners: The Ghilarducci Family (Chef/Proprietor: Michael; General Manager/Hostess: Gia; Executive Chef: Antonio)

"You never age at the table." This paraphrased Italian saying sums up the spirit of the Depot Hotel Restaurant and Garden—housed in a historic building, originally a hotel in 1870—and is what chef and proprietor Michael Ghilarducci says he loves most about the culture surrounding Italian cooking: loud laughter and debate, lots of wine drinking and storytelling, and simple enjoyment of the food before them.

Paradoxically, though, this is exactly what the delightful Ghilarducci family has done—grown up around the table. They lived over the restaurant for years, through the infancy of both the business and their own son, Antonio, now executive chef and provider of the recipes featured. (He and his wife now live with their young son upstairs—the baby's room is the former salumeria.)

After running several other restaurants in the Bay Area, the Ghilarduccis moved to the countryside to serve local Sonoma clientele, many historically Italian. "I learn more about cooking from old Italian men who come in here and tell me what I'm doing wrong than from school or any cookbook," laughs Antonio.

Though he downplays it, Antonio and his father both attended culinary school, and the son has worked in one of the best restaurants in the world—the nearby French Laundry. The Depot is a true family affair, with the father-son chef team and mother, Gia, the consummate hostess, manager, and pastry cook. Local products and the freshest of the fresh ingredients are a given—Michael used to pick watercress and catch local fish from the former creek that ran in front of the restaurant. They treasure the region's farm-focused roots.

"Before there were grapes or vineyards, this area was all cattle ranchers and pear farmers," Antonio says. Now their personal relationships with local farmers and purveyors inform the menu—a July pork shank dish with Italian couscous and summer vegetables was light in a way one never could've imagined. "My meat guy gave me these shanks and I knew I had to use them," Antonio says. They even make their own salumi and wine. Michael says he'll never retire.

"I taste caviar and truffles and drink great wine every day," Michael beams. "You'd have to be a millionaire to eat like we do and live life this way. Why give that up?"

Warm Calamari Salad on Crostini

(SERVES 8)

- 8 slices rustic Italian bread such as ciabatta, sliced ½ inch thick
- Extra-virgin olive oil
- Salt and pepper to taste
- 1 head garlic cut in half, plus 5 garlic cloves
- ¾ cup taggiasca or niçoise olives, pitted and washed
- 1 tomato
- 1 hot chili, either dried or whole Calabrian in oil
- 2 pounds small calamari, cleaned with tubes cut into rings, tentacles left whole
- Juice of 2 lemons
- 3 cups arugula leaves (wild preferred)

Preheat a grill or broiler to medium. Brush the bread with olive oil and sprinkle with salt and pepper. Grill until crunchy and golden (not black). Rub with the head of garlic and arrange on a serving platter.

In a food processor, add the olives, tomato, garlic cloves, and chili and process with olive oil to a rough (not smooth) paste. Set aside.

Heat a large sauté pan with olive oil until smoking. Working in batches to avoid overcrowding the pan, rapidly sauté a single layer of calamari at a time until just opaque. Transfer to a large bowl.

Add the olive mixture, lemon juice, more olive oil, and arugula to the calamari and toss well; check for seasoning. Divide evenly atop the crostini.

Grilled Quail Salad with Summer Pole Beans & Hazelnut Vinaigrette

(SERVES 8)

2 thyme sprigs
1 rosemary sprig
2 garlic cloves, thinly sliced
¼ cup extra-virgin olive oil
8 semi-boneless quail
1 pound yellow wax beans
1 pound Blue Lake beans or haricots verts
20 cherry tomatoes, thinly sliced
4 tablespoons salt, as needed for quail
¼ cup unsalted butter
¾ cup hazelnuts, crushed in half but not chopped
3 shallots, thinly sliced
1 tablespoon Dijon mustard
3 tablespoons sherry vinegar
Salt and pepper

Pick and chop the thyme and rosemary and put in a large bowl with the garlic and olive oil. Add the quail, cover completely, and set aside; do not refrigerate.

In a large pot of boiling salted water, blanch the beans until just tender, working in batches so the water doesn't lose its boil. Drain and put in ice water. Once the beans are chilled and drained, transfer to a large bowl. Add the tomatoes to the beans.

Shake off the excess marinade from the quail and put on a plate. Salt generously. Grill on medium-high heat until the juices from the breast run clear; set aside to rest.

In a medium saucepan, brown the butter over high heat to a nice golden color. Add the hazelnuts, shallots, mustard, and vinegar off the heat and season to taste with salt and pepper. Add any accumulated juices from the quail, then pour over the beans and tomatoes and toss well.

Arrange bean and tomato mixture on 8 plates. Top each with a grilled quail and, if desired, a drizzle of olive oil.

El Dorado Kitchen

405 First Street West
Sonoma, CA 95476
(707) 996-3030
www.eldoradosonoma.com
Chef: Armando Garcia

Tucked away in the back of the El Dorado Hotel, on the lovely Sonoma Square, lies a restaurant that feels both Sonoma and the Hamptons at once. With its cream-colored umbrellas and twisty wisteria trees, the patio of the El Dorado Kitchen (EDK, to those in the know) welcomes a modern country crowd. Businesspeople, wine country tourists, and ladies who lunch dine on elevated versions of classic dishes along with preparations that reflect chef Armando Garcia's raw talent, impressive résumé, and family heritage.

Growing up in Mexico, Garcia's family always had great food on the table—and most of it came from the family's own backyard. They raised chickens, goats, and cows; grew pumpkins, beans, and corn; and had fresh milk and eggs every day. And his mother, who he describes as his inspiration, ground that corn to make fresh tortillas for the family day in and day out.

Garcia's story of becoming a chef is not unusual: He began as a dishwasher in Napa and moved up when the chef in that kitchen asked for prep help. Since that fateful day, his career has blossomed. He went to culinary school and spent time in some of the best kitchens in the country—at Le Bernardin, Jean Georges, and Daniel Boulud in New York; Auberge du Soleil (page 138) in Rutherford; and Redd in Yountville. After a stint in Aspen, he is now at the helm of EDK and near his family (all now in the Napa Valley) once again.

Garcia deftly handles longtime EDK favorites and brings his own style through dishes like a beautiful, chilled corn soup and a mushroom *guarache* (Spanish for "sandal"), a crisp flatbread topped with mixed local mushrooms and doused in a bit of truffle oil. His braised lamb with local cranberry beans is a bit of a tribute to this dish from his childhood. And like when he was a kid, those ingredients all come from very nearby the kitchen. Garcia's Roasted Petaluma Chicken Salad (recipe here) presents itself impressively and delivers on taste: a tower of plump chunks of local chicken and gorgeous heirloom tomatoes, topped with delicate, crispy onion rings—the perfect, and complete, lunch dish.

Beet Salad

(SERVES 4)

For the roasted beets:

3 each baby Chiogga, baby gold, and baby red beets, washed and tops trimmed
2 tablespoons canola oil
Salt and pepper to taste

For the goat cheese mousse:

½ cup goat cheese (preferably Laura Chenel's Chèvre)
2 tablespoons olive oil
Salt and pepper to taste

For the citrus vinaigrette:

1 California orange
1 Ruby Red grapefruit
Juice of 1 lime
Juice of 1 lemon
1 cup canola oil
¼ cup extra-virgin olive oil

For the arugula:

4 cups of arugula, washed

Preheat oven to 375°F.

In a small bowl, toss baby beets with canola oil, salt, and pepper. Place seasoned beets in a shallow casserole dish with 1 cup of water and cover tightly with foil. Roast in preheated oven for 45 minutes or until tender throughout. Let cool, then peel and quarter.

To make the mousse, fold together goat cheese and olive oil with a spatula until smooth. Season with salt and pepper to taste.

To make the vinaigrette, peel and segment the orange and grapefruit; set aside the segments for plating and reserve the juice. In a small saucepan over high heat, reduce the juice to ¼ cup and let cool. Place the citrus juice in a mixing bowl with the lime and lemon juices and slowly whisk in canola oil to emulsify. Finish dressing with olive oil.

Toss the beets with the citrus vinaigrette and adjust seasoning as necessary. Remove the dressed beets from the viniagrette and set aside. Toss arugula in remainder of vinaigrette. Plate beets in 4 shallow bowls, add 5 dots goat cheese mousse to each bowl of beets, top with dressed arugula (approximately 1 cup per plate), and garnish with citrus segments.

Roasted Petaluma Chicken Salad

(SERVES 4)

For the sherry vinaigrette:

2 tablespoons Dijon mustard
1 garlic clove
½ cup sherry vinegar
¾ cup canola oil
¼ cup extra-virgin olive oil

For the salad:

4 each air-chilled, boneless, skin-on chicken legs and thighs
4 mixed heirloom tomatoes (such as Spike, Black Krim, Brandywine Yellow, and Green Zebra), cut into bite-size chunks
1–2 cucumbers, peeled, seeded, and sliced
1 red onion, peeled and sliced thin
4 cups arugula

For the onion rings:

2 Walla Walla onions, sliced into ¼-inch rings
Approximately ½ cup buttermilk
Mixture of 2 parts flour and 1 part semolina
Oil for frying

To make the vinaigrette, whisk all ingredients to combine. Alternatively, you may place all ingredients in a jar with a tight lid, and shake the jar until the vinaigrette is emulsified.

To prepare the chicken, preheat oven to 400°F. Season chicken pieces with salt. In a hot, ovenproof sauté pan, sear chicken skin-side down for 90 seconds, and then finish in the preheated oven until cooked through (when juices run clear). Remove from oven and let rest for 5 minutes. Dice chicken into bite-size (1-inch) pieces.

To make the onion rings, toss the onion slices with buttermilk and dredge individual rings in the flour-semolina mixture. Fry the coated onion rings in pot of oil heated to 350°F until golden brown and crispy.

To plate, toss roasted chicken, tomatoes, cucumbers, red onions, and arugula with sherry vinaigrette (taste for seasoning). Mound salad artfully in a tall stack on each plate and garnish each serving with 7 or 8 crispy onion rings.

Estate

400 West Spain Street
Sonoma, CA 95476
(707) 933-3663
www.estate-sonoma.com
Owner/Proprietor: Sondra Bernstein
Chef/Managing Partner: John Toulze

Although Sondra Bernstein spent years as director of operations at Sonoma's Viansa Winery & Marketplace, self-described as "a tribute to the early Italian immigrants who brought their winemaking traditions to Sonoma Valley," when she left and first opened her own restaurant (The Girl and the Fig, page 82) she wanted to do something non-Italian.

With Estate, Bernstein returns to her early professional roots in a gloriously homey way. The space previously housed the popular California cuisine–focused General's Daughter—the name a nod to the family home that had occupied the gorgeous Victorian for more than a hundred years—and is

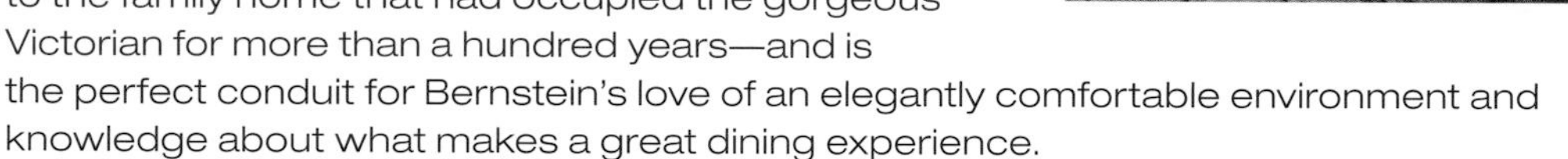

the perfect conduit for Bernstein's love of an elegantly comfortable environment and knowledge about what makes a great dining experience.

The fact that the restaurant is Italian makes sense not only on historical and personal levels, but also on a modern one. In 2009 Sonoma became the first US city to be designated a "Cittaslow"—meaning "slow city" in Italian—which is an extension of Italy's Slow Food movement. Cittaslow celebrates the preservation of tradition and the heritage of small towns, and perhaps most importantly, of their commitment to sustainability, artisan products, and local foods.

At Estate the food is Italian, but the space feels totally Bernstein with its spacious patio, inviting dining room, and warm colors all around. Diners may select any of the a la carte menu items or opt for the family-style dinner for a minimum of two people. The prix-fixe menu rotates weekly and always includes an antipasti (starter), primi (first course, often pasta), secondi (main dish), contorni (side), and dolce (dessert)—four courses for a modest price.

Ranging from house-made pastas and lovely pizzas to hearty main dishes—all with beautiful farm-fresh ingredients—the fare at Estate clearly bears the mark of the Bernstein–John Toulze partnership but with a strong Italian core. The fun, easygoing enjoyment of the land and products endemic to a particular region is one of Bernstein's hallmarks—she also is a major Europhile—and explains the fabulous selection of grappas and grappa-related liqueurs available at the establishment's "grappa bar." Flights are even available for the strong-tongued. Additionally, Toulze makes his own salumi and offers occasional classes on how to do it.

Described by Bernstein as a way "to explore the wonderful flavors of Italy as they relate to Sonoma," Estate is just that. But it's even more. It is an expression of the

business partners' relationship having come full circle—Toulze and Bernstein first met in an Italian-focused setting, when he worked for her at Viansa at the young age of nineteen. It is a celebration of family and fun and heritage. And it is the latest in a petite collection of small-town restaurants that welcomes diners to experience what the land has to offer, every night of the week.

Mixed Chicory Salad with White Balsamic Vinaigrette

(SERVES 6)

For the vinaigrette:

¼ cup white balsamic vinegar
½ cup extra-virgin olive oil
Salt and pepper to taste

For the salad:

1 bunch mizuna, cleaned and large stems removed
1 head radicchio, cleaned and torn into 3-inch pieces
2 heads endive, leaves removed
2 cups arugula
1 head frisée, cleaned and core removed
½ cup fresh pomegranate seeds
2 blood oranges, cut into supremes or thin slices
2 navel oranges, cut into supremes or thin slices
Salt and pepper to taste

To prepare the vinaigrette, whisk together the vinegar and the olive oil. Season with salt and pepper to taste.

To prepare the salad, combine the mizuna, radicchio, endive, arugula, frisée, pomegranate seeds, and citrus with the vinaigrette in a large mixing bowl. Toss well and season with salt and pepper to taste. Distribute evenly among 6 plates.

Sweet Gem Romaine and Vella Dry Jack with Caper Vinaigrette

(SERVES 6)

For the vinaigrette (yields 1½ cups):

¼ cup champagne vinegar
¾ cup blended oil
2 tablespoons diced shallots
2 tablespoons fresh thyme leaves
2 tablespoons chopped capers
Salt and freshly ground white pepper
Pinch of sugar
Juice of 1 lemon

For the salad:

¼ cup canola oil
6 tablespoons capers, drained and patted dry
6 heads Sweet Gem romaine or other good-quality romaine lettuce, cut in half and washed
Salt and freshly cracked black pepper
30 slices (about ¼ pound) Vella Dry Jack, sliced with a vegetable peeler
¼ cup caperberries
½ medium red onion, sliced thin
12 white Spanish anchovies, drained (optional)

To make the vinaigrette, whisk the vinegar, oil, shallots, thyme, and capers together in a bowl. Season to taste with the salt, pepper, sugar, and lemon juice. The vinaigrette will keep in a sealed container in the refrigerator for up to 1 week. Whisk before using.

Heat the canola oil in a small sauté pan over medium heat. Add the capers to the hot oil and fry until they are crispy. Strain the capers and place them on a paper towel to drain. Set aside.

Place the lettuce halves in a bowl and toss with half of the vinaigrette, salt, and pepper. Place two halves of the Sweet Gem onto each chilled plate.

Sprinkle the fried capers, 5 slices of Vella Dry Jack, and caperberries over each portion. Add the red onion slices and anchovies on top and garnish with the remaining vinaigrette around the plate to taste.

The Fremont Diner

2698 Fremont Drive
Sonoma, CA 95476
(707) 938-7370
www.thefremontdiner.com
Chef/Owner: Chad Harris

The Fremont Diner describes itself as "a place where serious southern food is done with distinct local sensibility," which is absolutely true. But what this description misses is the uniqueness of the place and the sheer love people have for it. To say it is adored is not an exaggeration, and the fervor is warranted. It's like the cult hero of Sonoma restaurants, for its maddeningly good comfort foods, funky decor, indoor-outdoor seating, and fresh-from-the-farm ingredients.

California and Mississippi native Chad Harris never wanted his own restaurant—not really, he says. Fortunately for all of us, the Bay Area kid with a love of southern food and Americana was intrigued when his mother told him about the For Sale sign on the long-abandoned roadside diner. So he submitted his mission statement for a business to the city and beat out thirty other people for the property.

"It all stems from my road trips through Italy and my time in South Carolina," explains Harris, sharing his love of the truck stops and mom-and-pop joints that dotted the roads in some of his favorite parts of the world. "I wanted to give people the same experience here that those places gave me."

Open just until 3 p.m. daily (and until 4 p.m. on Sundays), the Fremont Diner's fare takes a Nor-Cal approach to "southern Americana" classics like biscuits and gravy, hearty breakfast hashes, burgers, shakes and floats, chicken and waffles, muffulettas, po'boys, and fritters of all sorts. The diner's Sonoma location becomes evident in its ingredients—many of which come from the diner's own farm out back, which is replete with 250 egg-laying chickens, pigs, and a wide variety of fruits and vegetables—as well as in dishes like the Hangtown Fry, featuring local Drake's Bay oysters, and "figs in a blanket," for the mascot fruit of Sonoma. Everything, it should be said, is wildly delicious.

"If it doesn't come from our own farm, it comes from someone I know," Harris explains. Personal connections and generational relationships are an important part of his vision for the diner—he hopes to carry on the tradition started by the original proprietor of the roadside joint in 1965 (who still lives next door): She watched kids grow up at the restaurant.

"I feel like it's already happening," Harris enthuses, sharing that he's with the Fremont Diner for the long haul. "Definitely the farthest I'll ever get from this place is in a rocking chair out back, next to my smoker."

Persimmon Salad

(SERVES 4)

For the dressing (yields 1 cup):

1/3 cup apple cider vinegar
2/3 cup olive oil
1 tablespoon Dijon mustard
Salt and pepper to taste

For the salad:

Seeds from 1 pomegranate
1 head radicchio, core removed and leaves chopped
1 head escarole, core removed and leaves chopped
1–2 Fuyu persimmons, sliced
3 ounces blue cheese, crumbled (approximately ½ cup)
¼ cup walnuts
4 pieces cooked bacon, chopped into small pieces

To make the dressing, combine all ingredients in a jelly jar and shake well until completely combined.

Combine all salad ingredients in a large bowl; toss with hands to combine. Drizzle dressing over the top to your taste; toss again to incorporate. Divide salad evenly among 4 plates to serve.

The Fremont Diner's Famous Ham Biscuit

(SERVES 6–8)

We cure our own ham here at the diner, and recommend using your favorite style of ham in this biscuit.

For the quince-bay jelly:

3 pounds quince
Water
1 bay leaf
Sugar to taste

For the famous biscuits:

2 cups all-purpose flour
1 tablespoon aluminum-free or homemade* baking powder (*combine equal parts cream of tartar and baking soda)
¾ teaspoon salt
½ cup unsalted butter
1½ cups buttermilk

Special equipment:

2½-inch biscuit cutter

Your favorite mustard to taste
9–12 ounces prepared ham, cut into slices or biscuit-size chunks, to your preference

To prepare the jelly, cut quince into small pieces and place pieces in a pot. Fill pot with water to just cover quince; add bay leaf. Meanwhile, place a small plate in the freezer.

Simmer the quince until liquid has taken on a rosy color. Strain pulp and liquid; discard pulp. Fill pot with equal volume measurement of sugar and liquid. Simmer until a small spoonful of the jelly passes the "freezer test." (Spoon a small amount of jelly onto the frozen plate; it is finished when the spoon makes a smooth line through the jelly and it doesn't flow back together.)

To make the biscuits, mix flour, baking powder, and salt in a medium bowl. Cut up cold butter into small pieces. Put flour and butter in a Cuisinart to mix, or if mixing by hand, place in the bowl. Pulse quickly until the butter is in pea-size pieces, then put back into bowl. (If mixing by hand, either use a pastry cutter or blend with hands until it resembles cornflakes.) Add buttermilk and stir until a wet but manageable dough comes together. If the dough is too dry, keep adding buttermilk until it comes together. If the dough is too wet, just add a little flour at a time until the dough is more manageable.

Flour the work surface. Roll out dough using a generous amount of flour. Fold dough over and roll again. Repeat twice. Dough may be rather wet, so keep adding flour until it forms a smooth, workable dough.

Preheat oven to 400°F. Roll dough 1-inch thick and cut into biscuits, using a biscuit cutter. Place biscuits on a cookie sheet; they should almost touch. Bake in the preheated oven for 20 minutes. Remove from oven and cool on a baking rack until easy to handle.

To assemble a ham biscuit, split a biscuit horizontally in half. Spread your favorite mustard on one inner side of the biscuit, and spoon and spread prepared quince-bay jelly on the other inner side of the biscuit to taste. Add ham pieces to taste to make a biscuit "sandwich" and enjoy. Make as many ham biscuits as there are hungry people awaiting them—as a starter, side, or several per person, for breakfast or lunch or on their own.

The Girl and the Fig

110 West Spain Street
Sonoma, CA 95476
(707) 938-3634
www.thegirlandthefig.com
Owner/Proprietor: Sondra Bernstein
Chef/Managing Partner: John Toulze

Sondra Bernstein, the girl behind The Girl and the Fig, has a huge heart, a true entrepreneur's spirit, and a work ethic to match. She never seems to slow down, even after three restaurants and two cookbooks of her own, managing what she calls "The Farm Project," and blogging, tweeting, catering, and canning. And there is no sign of her slowing down anytime soon.

The Girl and the Fig is her first and most famous restaurant, named to represent her ("the girl") and a dominant symbol of the region ("the fig"). While sitting under a fig tree pondering her business plan, the idea struck her.

"The fig is a symbol for Sonoma: the bounty, the passion, the joie de vivre," Bernstein explains. "But it's also erotic, exotic, and incredibly versatile. It can be dessert, savory, in salads, or with cheese, dried or fresh, or even used in cocktails." And the girl uses the precious fruit in all of those ways, and more, on her menu.

But it is not just figs on offer. Philadelphia-raised Bernstein also has a major affinity for France, her love evident in many menu items. Like at Estate (page 76), she has a similar rotating prix fixe, the three-course Bistro Plat Du Jour. Pastis-scented steamed mussels, *croques monsieur,* and a delightful duck confit all make appearances on the Fig's menu. Vibrant heirloom radishes served simply, unadorned, with anchovy butter and gray sea salt, seem to epitomize the French-Californian approach. Many of the ingredients come from the restaurant's own farm (hence, the aforementioned "project") and highlight the state's bounteous seasons. Bernstein says, "I want to taste the earth in a carrot, and I want to taste the grass in a beautiful cheese."

Dining at The Girl and the Fig feels like dining in an old favorite restaurant, even if it's your first time there. Comfortable booths and tables with bright, warm paintings fill the space, and the patio, with its twinkly lights, ivied walls, and billowy canopies, feels like a charmed, beautifully styled dinner party at a friend's house. You would never guess that Bernstein's first restaurant job was as a waitress at TGI Friday's—but it's where she learned that she loved the "vibrant, crazy" restaurant business, which she describes as "like being at a party all day long." Stints in various restaurants, coupled with a degree in culinary management, led her to this place, to her muse, the fig.

"The fig is a really precious fruit," Bernstein explains, given its short season, its almost magical insides, and the way it seems to symbolize the brevity of life. "You can wait and wait, and eat too many when they finally appear, and before you know it, they're gone."

Grilled Fig & Arugula Salad

(SERVES 6)

For the vinaigrette:

1 cup ruby port
3 dried Black Mission figs
¼ cup red wine vinegar
½ tablespoon minced shallots
¼ cup blended oil
Salt and pepper to taste

For the salad:

½ cup diced pancetta
12 fresh figs, halved
6 bunches baby arugula
1 cup pecans, toasted
1 cup crumbled goat cheese (preferably Laura Chenel's Chèvre)
Freshly ground black pepper to taste

To prepare the vinaigrette, pour the port in a bowl, add the figs, and rehydrate until soft. Transfer the port and figs to a saucepan. Reduce the port over medium heat to ½ cup, about 5–7 minutes. Transfer the port mixture to a food processor and add the vinegar. Puree until smooth. Add the shallots and slowly whisk in the oil. Season to taste with salt and pepper.

To prepare the salad, sauté the pancetta in a small sauté pan over medium heat until the pancetta is crisp. Set the pancetta aside, reserving the "oil." Brush the figs with the pancetta "oil." Grill the figs for 45 seconds on each side. In a stainless-steel bowl, toss the arugula, pecans, pancetta, and goat cheese with the vinaigrette.

To serve, divide the salad among 6 chilled plates and surround it with the grilled figs. Grind the pepper over each salad.

Heirloom Tomato & Watermelon Salad

(SERVES 6)

For the vinaigrette:

1 medium yellow tomato, blanched, peeled, and seeded
1 tablespoon Dijon mustard
1 tablespoon champagne vinegar
½ cup extra-virgin olive oil
Salt and white pepper to taste

For the salad:

½ cup crumbled feta cheese
3 tablespoons extra-virgin olive oil
2 pounds assorted heirloom tomatoes, sliced into ½-inch pieces
1 pound seedless watermelon, rind removed and sliced into ½- x 2-inch rounds
2 tablespoons fresh oregano leaves for garnish
Sea salt to taste

To prepare the vinaigrette, place the yellow tomato in a blender. On medium speed, add the mustard and then the vinegar. Slowly add ½ cup olive oil. Taste and season with salt and white pepper as needed and set aside.

In a separate bowl, mix the crumbled feta with 3 tablespoons olive oil.

To serve, divide the heirloom tomato slices and watermelon slices equally among 6 plates. When plating, alternate the slices and garnish with a bit of feta. Drizzle the vinaigrette over each portion and garnish with the oregano leaves. Add a touch of sea salt to the salad if desired.

Harvest Moon Cafe

487 First Street West
Sonoma, CA 95476
(707) 933.8160
www.harvestmooncafesonoma.com
Chefs/Owners: Nick and Jen Demarest

Dining at the Harvest Moon Cafe in Sonoma feels like dining at the comfortable home of a good friend—one who really knows how to cook. Husband-wife, chef–pastry chef duo Nick and Jen Demarest are gracious, talented young cooks and owners who turn out delicious dinner night after night (plus brunch on Sundays) while also balancing catering for special events and the raising of their adorable young daughter.

Originally from Texas and New York respectively, the couple met at The Culinary Institute of America (CIA) in Hyde Park, but their work in restaurants began

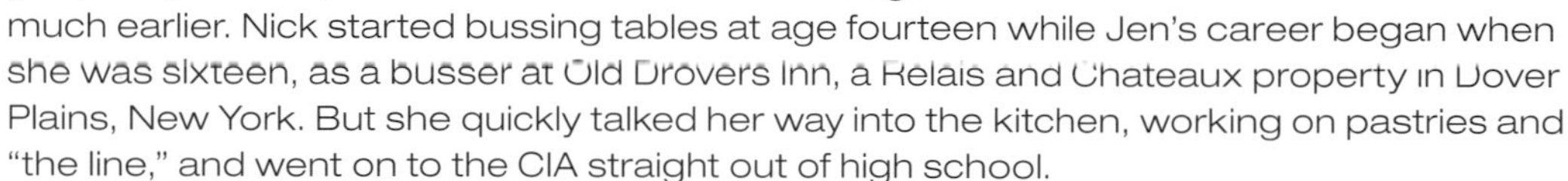

much earlier. Nick started bussing tables at age fourteen while Jen's career began when she was sixteen, as a busser at Old Drovers Inn, a Relais and Chateaux property in Dover Plains, New York. But she quickly talked her way into the kitchen, working on pastries and "the line," and went on to the CIA straight out of high school.

The two traveled extensively, including spending time in Cyprus, where Nick was the private chef for the US ambassador to the country; working for legendary chef David Tanis in Santa Fe; and then in the kitchen of Alice Waters's Chez Panisse, in Berkeley, California. Their style is simple, "not molecular gastronomy," and a mix of all of these experiences—and it shows.

The cafe's weekly changing menu features just a handful of starters and salads and a short list of main dishes, highlighting Italian, Middle Eastern, Southeast Asian, and Californian flavors and preparations. Diners may have crispy fried pale-green tomatoes paired with luscious fresh bright-red tomatoes (from one of the three local farms they work with) in the same meal as a beautiful Cal-Mediterranean-style bouillabaisse, absolutely filled with plump local shrimp, mussels, and whitefish in a subtle saffron broth.

Savory items are complemented by delectable meal-ending and reimagined classic sweets from Jen—such as a treatment of s'mores where a gigantic homemade marshmallow envelopes the layers of chocolate, graham, and amazing peanut butter mousse, hidden inside. When it comes to wine, the Demarests offer an accessible wine list that, unusually, changes each week as well. With many by-the-glass options on such a short list, Nick enjoys offering wines that people might not often see—and he purposely does not have a sommelier on staff.

The place named for the agricultural harvest, for its location in the "valley of the moon," and for the casual quality that dining in a "cafe" evokes has become a favorite of local chefs, Sonoma residents, and visitors to wine country.

Mozzarella, Corona Bean & Roasted Radicchio Salad with Prosciutto, Saba & White Truffle Oil

(SERVES 4–6)

For the beans:

1 cup dried beans (Borlotti, cannellini, or corona beans work best)
½ yelllow onion, peeled and chopped
1 carrot, peeled and chopped
1 stalk celery, chopped
Spoonful of chopped garlic
Pinch of red pepper flakes
2 bay leaves
Salt to taste
½ teaspoon each chopped parsley, chives, and marjoram
Sherry vinegar to taste

For the salad:

3 heads radicchio
Olive oil
¼ cup balsamic vinegar or to taste
Salt and pepper to taste
2–3 (4-ounce) balls fresh mozzarella
4–6 slices prosciutto
White truffle oil to taste
Saba or reduced balsamic vinegar to taste

Soak beans overnight in cold water. Drain water from beans.

Pour beans into a pot and cover with water. Add onion, carrot, celery, garlic, red pepper flakes, and bay leaves and bring to a boil. Reduce to a simmer and cook until beans are tender. Once beans are cooked, add salt to taste. Cool beans and season with chopped herbs. Add sherry vinegar to taste.

Preheat oven to 400°F.

Remove any wilted outer leaves of the radicchio. Cut radicchio into sixths or eighths lengthwise, leaving stem attached. Lay radicchio in a rimmed baking dish, drizzle with olive oil and approximately ¼ cup balsamic vinegar, and sprinkle with salt and fresh black pepper. Bake for 12–15 minutes, until leaves are wilted and slightly charred.

Slice mozzarella balls into ¼-inch slices. Divide slices evenly between serving plates and sprinkle each slice with salt. Put a couple spoonfuls of beans on each plate, with some beans on top of the mozzarella and some around it. Arrange radicchio wedges and drape prosciutto slices around the plates. Drizzle with white truffle oil and saba vinegar.

Beet, Citrus & Avocado Salad with Albacore Crudo & Ginger-Jalapeño Vinaigrette

(SERVES 4–6)

For the beets:

15 baby beets
2 tablespoons plus ¼ cup olive oil
2 tablespoons water
2 tablespoons salt
1 tablespoon sherry vinegar
Salt to taste

For the vinaigrette:

3 tablespoons peeled and minced ginger
1 lime, zested and juiced
1 seeded jalapeño
1 shallot
2 tablespoons white wine vinegar
⅓ cup olive oil
Pinch of salt

For the salad:

1¼ pounds albacore tuna
2 oranges
2 grapefruits
2 avocados
Salt to taste
1 bunch mint

Preheat oven to 450°F.

Place beets in a pan with 2 tablespoons olive oil, 2 tablespoons water, and 2 tablespoons salt. Cover and roast about 1 hour, or until tender and can be easily pierced with a paring knife. Allow to cool, then peel. Slice and marinate with ¼ cup olive oil, sherry vinegar, and salt to taste.

Place ginger, lime zest and juice, jalapeño, shallot, and white wine vinegar in a blender and blend on high. Pour mixture into a bowl and whisk in olive oil and a pinch of salt to finish the vinaigrette.

Place albacore tuna on a clean work surface and trim any bloodline off. Place the loin bloodline-side down on the cutting board and, using a sharp knife, cut in half lengthwise. Cut on a bias, making thin slices. Set aside in refrigerator.

Peel the oranges and grapefruit, removing all of the white pith. Segment the citrus and set aside.

To assemble the salad, place beet slices on each plate. Cut avocado in half, remove seed, and with a spoon, scoop a few pieces on each plate. Place some of the albacore slices on the plates. Sprinkle avocado and fish with salt and put a few segments of orange and grapefruit on the plates. Stir the vinaigrette well and spoon over all the salad components. Chop some mint and sprinkle over the top.

STONE EDGE FARM

PO Box 487, Sonoma, CA 95476
(707) 935-6520 · www.stoneedgefarm.com
Proprietor: Mac McQuown; Culinary Director: John McReynolds

"It's important to become acquainted with the natural landscape around you," says John McReynolds, culinary director at Stone Edge Farm. As a fifth-generation Californian with more than twenty years spent living in the area, "I have a pretty good sense of the plants and animals, air and seasonality, and culinary traditions of this part of the world."

Stone Edge Farm is technically an estate, but the term doesn't seem right to adequately describe all that goes on there. The farm is also a gorgeous winery and olive oil producer as well as culinary educator, through the work of McReynolds. After a decade as co-owner and chef at Sonoma's Cafe La Haye (page 64), he ventured out on his own and pursued a new sort of adventure on the farm.

The culinarian hails from a family of hunters and fishermen always "interested in securing our own food." He loves the resurgence of interest in food and connecting with the food source. He conducts workshops on how to make natural plant dyes and loves to harvest his own acorns from oak trees on the property to process into acorn flour and use in his cooking. McReynolds reveres the "edible landscape" around him.

"There is so much flora and fauna in Sonoma that can be used in your food," he enthuses, sharing the exciting reminders of the history of human frugality and of making use of available "products."

What's most important, according to McReynolds, is checking out what's available and endemic to one's particular area. In Japan, succulents, seaweeds, and grasses in tidal areas are all important parts of the native diet—"they never lost contact with their wild edibles," he says—just as in Sonoma, oak acorns, wild greens like watercress and miner's lettuce, mushrooms, endless herbs, and even seaweed from the Pacific Ocean's vast coastline can be harvested for consumption. McReynolds even uses the calendula that grows all over the farm's vineyards in his gnocchi, giving the dumplings a beautiful saffron color.

Moving to work on a farm is a logical step for a chef, he says, especially one like him, who believes in "cooking simply, letting the products reveal their nature."

Because Stone Edge is a small, private estate, all visitors must make an appointment to see the operation in action—and they should. Afterwards, with McReynolds's love of coaxing natural ingredients into the best realization of themselves as an inspiration, return home and discover the gems in your own natural landscape.

LaSalette Restaurant

452 First Street East, Suite H
Sonoma, CA 95476
(707) 938-1927
www.lasalette-restaurant.com
Owner/Chef: Manuel Azevedo

Stepping into LaSalette Restaurant—one of only a few Portuguese restaurants in California—feels as though you've entered someone's coastal country home. The fire of the open, wood-burning oven beckons you into the butter-yellow-walled space where, once seated, you quickly settle in with a glass of *vinho verde* and insightful recommendations from a friendly staff member about the evening's dishes.

The restaurant is named for chef and owner Manuel Azevedo's mother (LaSalette is her family name) and is a tribute to her traditional, peasant-style Portuguese cuisine—with oftentimes ethereal, contemporary versions of it. *Cozinha novo Portuguesa*—or "new Portuguese cuisine"—is what Azevedo calls it, best defined as a marriage between classic Portuguese flavors, modern preparations, and local California products. While surprising to some, the style is really not a stretch, Azevedo says. Tomatoes, peppers, cheeses, olive oil, and artisanal meats are all prevalent in Portuguese cookery and shape the food scene in the Sonoma region today.

Azevedo's father was a dairy farmer, a profession that spurred the family's move to the United States from the Azores when Manuel was only two. They settled in Sonoma—similar in many ways to his homeland, with farming chief among them. "I grew up as if I was still back in the islands," he says. Portuguese food was simply a given for the chef as a child. But as a teenager, after working as a dishwasher in the local rib joint and graduating to the position of chef in just six months, Azevedo got the restaurant bug—and started to look at food, especially that of his childhood, in a new way.

His compact frame and quiet charm belies the huge pride he has in his native cuisine and its bold and simultaneously classic comfort-food flavors. The perfect harmony of a chorizo-crusted scallop with stewed fennel, Japanese sweet potatoes, and the loveliest heirloom tomatoes is just one example of his contemporary treatment of native flavors. It tastes of the sea and the farm in an incredibly balanced way, and will stay with the diner for a long, long time—just as Azevedo hopes the diner will have a lasting appreciation of the beauty and deliciousness of his beloved Portuguese cuisine.

Citrus-Cured Baby Octopus with Fennel & Endive Salad

Polvo Bebé Curado em Sumo de Limão com Salada de Funcho e Endívias

(SERVES 4)

Octopus is a popular choice year-round in Portugal, but it's great paired with citrus in the winter or spring when these fruits are at their seasonal best. In this recipe the citrus flavor really sets off both the octopus and the salad to give the dish a sweet, tangy, and fruity punch. The trick is to cook the octopus quickly on very high heat, regardless of your cooking method. Baby octopus is typically available by order from most fishmongers and quality supermarkets. It is often frozen—so it's widely available but not always displayed in markets because of its specialized interest.

For the octopus:

1 pound baby octopus
2 tablespoons orange juice
2 tablespoons lemon juice
2 tablespoons Madeira
1 teaspoon granulated sugar
2 teaspoons balsamic vinegar
2 tablespoons dry red wine
2 garlic cloves, minced
1 teaspoon fine sea salt
Pinch of red pepper flakes

For the vinaigrette:

½ teaspoon (about ½ mandarin) mandarin orange zest
3 tablespoons mandarin orange juice
2 tablespoons minced shallots
2 teaspoons lemon juice
1 teaspoon Worcestershire sauce
½ teaspoon piri piri (a Portuguese hot sauce) or other hot sauce
⅓ cup white wine vinegar
¼ cup extra-virgin olive oil
1 garlic clove, minced
½ teaspoon freshly ground black pepper
½ teaspoon fine sea salt
1 tablespoon chopped parsley

For the salad:

2 fennel bulbs
2 Belgian endives
1 shallot, thinly sliced
Mandarin orange segments
Chopped chives
Freshly ground black pepper
Piri piri sauce (optional)

To prepare the octopus, cut the mantle (head) off the octopuses and cut them in half lengthwise. Remove base of mantle where eyes are from each octopus; discard base and eyes. Cut tentacles in half so that there are 2 sets of 4 tentacles for each octopus. Remove the dark-colored beak from the base of the tentacles (it is in the center); discard beaks. Separate tentacles with a sharp knife and wash mantle pieces and tentacles thoroughly in water. Combine with the remaining octopus ingredients and marinate in the refrigerator for 8 hours, mixing every 2–3 hours.

To make the vinaigrette, combine the ingredients in a blender for about 10–15 seconds. Refrigerate mixture for at least 1 hour to bring out the flavors.

To assemble the salad, cut fennel lengthwise and then cut the halves into thin slices (ideally using a mandoline). Cut endives in half lengthwise and then cut ⅜-inch-thick strips from the halves crosswise. Place endive, fennel, shallot, and orange slices in a bowl and add the vinaigrette. Mix and refrigerate for 5–10 minutes to develop the flavor.

To serve, remove the salad from the refrigerator. Toss the chives into the salad and season the salad with pepper. Position a portion of salad on the side of each plate. Flash bake the marinated octopus at 500°F for 1 to 2 minutes or grill rapidly on high heat. Remove octopus from the oven or grill and immediately distribute among the plates. Serve with piri piri sauce if desired.

Ledson Hotel & Centre Du Vin

480 First Street East
Sonoma, CA 95476
(707) 996-9779
www.ledsonhotel.com
Owner: Steve Ledson; Chef: Justin Bruckert

The Ledson Hotel's Centre Du Vin feels like a cafe in a small, boutique Parisian hotel, with its limestone facade and wrought-iron accents—architecture more like what you would see on the Champs Elysees instead of the Sonoma Square. Outfitted with stone flooring, a marble fireplace, and red-and-white bistro-style wicker chairs, this French-inspired establishment is overseen by Arizona-native chef Justin Bruckert, who got his start in his grandmother's kitchen long before eventually studying culinary arts at the Art Institute of Phoenix.

After coming to Sonoma with his family, Bruckert discovered that wine country has a profound culture of food and wine—and that he loves the farmers' market. His seasonal menus showcase classic dishes and ingredients such as coq au vin, rabbit, and roasted root vegetables. He feels no need to use "trendy techniques" and wants his food to speak for itself. "Simple is delicious," as Bruckert says, explaining his commitment to making delicious comfort food.

He also enjoys the region's pinot noir and petite syrah, and says, "Cooking with good wine means there will be good food on the menu." Centre du Vin's wine list consists primarily of local wines, with a robust selection of estate-grown wines from Ledson's own winery.

Bruckert is a new-to-Sonoma chef who enjoys connecting with local sourcing. "It's inspiring to see how food evolves from the farms, rivers, and ranches to the plates of our guests," he shares, reflecting on the high quality of buying organic and the commitment to supporting local farmers, which he terms "a win-win situation."

So go, after a stroll along the square, and enjoy a glass of wine and a plate of French comfort food at the counter or at one of the many tables in the Centre du Vin—it will feel like a virtual trip to Paris.

Tender Butter Leaf Lettuce, Sliced Green Apple, Gorgonzola & Walnuts with Champagne Vinaigrette

(SERVES 4)

For the champagne vinaigrette:

1 garlic clove, finely chopped
2 tablespoons Dijon mustard
¼ cup champagne vinegar
2 tablespoons freshly squeezed lemon juice
2 tablespoons honey
2–3 dashes Tabasco
½ teaspoon kosher salt
½ teaspoon black pepper, freshly ground
½ cup extra-virgin olive oil

For the salad:

1 head butter lettuce
6 tablespoons champagne vinaigrette
¼ cup walnut halves
1 green apple (or your favorite variety), sliced
¼ cup crumbled Gorgonzola

Whisk together the vinaigrette ingredients (minus the olive oil) in a large bowl. Slowly whisk in the olive oil until the dressing is emulsified. Alternatively, you can combine all the ingredients in a blender or a food processor and puree until smooth.

Mix the lettuce with the dressing; top the salad with walnuts, apple, and Gorgonzola; and serve.

Santé Restaurant

100 Boyes Boulevard
Sonoma, CA 95476
(707) 938-9000
www.fairmont.com/sonoma
Chef: Andrew Cain

Cauliflower custard, served in a perfectly snipped brown eggshell, topped with a delicate spoonful of caviar: This is the kind of dish that might greet you when you sit down to dinner at Santé Restaurant at the Fairmont Sonoma Mission Inn and Spa.

Absolute elegance is expressed by the food at this Michelin-starred restaurant, nestled in the California mission-style hotel that seems to be the real-life expression of your best daydreams, but the relaxed service makes you feel immediately at home. Any notion of stuffiness is tossed into the neighboring courtyard as the waitstaff confess their favorite menu items and joke comfortably with customers, while presenting every dish with precision and describing each paired wine with complete finesse.

Chef Andrew Cain grew up in Maryland, and his affinity for seafood is apparent on the menu. His treatment of fish is sublime: Even his Grown-up Mac & Cheese features lobster (and truffles, delightfully). Like other chefs in the area, Cain spent time at The French Laundry, and he describes his style of cooking as "based on local products with French technique." Local products have always been part of his life—as a child, he enjoyed fresh raspberries from his grandfather's Wisconsin patch and honey from his local bees.

Cain's blend of simple childhood pleasures and esteemed training translates to the Santé experience of the complex and seemingly simple at once. The seasonal chilled pea soup instantly becomes something you want every day of your life—it tastes like popping open a pea pod and sampling its contents while still standing in the garden. In an appetizer that features a duo of foie gras preparations, pickled local strawberries adorn a torchon, while a lovely confit of rhubarb accompanies the seared version.

The restaurant's placement in Sonoma is evident. "There are not many places in the world where you have local farmers, fishmongers, and ranchers all in the same place," Cain says. "A lot of what you are eating tonight was picked this morning"—even the cauliflower in that special custard.

Salad of Garden Cucumber & Heirloom Radishes with Champagne Vinaigrette & Mint Tzatziki

(SERVES 6)

For the tzatziki:

¾ cup organic plain yogurt
¼ cup mint oil
2 tablespoons finely chopped cucumber, skin and seeds removed before chopping
1 teaspoon salt

For the salad:

1 English cucumber, thinly sliced (if available, a mandoline is the preferred tool for thinly slicing these ingredients)
1 Armenian cucumber, thinly sliced
3 lemon cucumbers, peeled and quartered
1 black radish, thinly sliced
1 flambeau radish, thinly sliced
1 breakfast radish, thinly sliced
1 small watermelon radish, peeled and cut into 1-inch batonettes
3 tablespoons champagne vinegar
6 tablespoons extra-virgin olive oil
1 tablespoon salt
36 pieces of micro-mint or mint tips

To make the tzatziki, combine the yogurt, mint oil, and chopped cucumber and season with salt.

To prepare the salad, dress the cucumbers and radishes with the champagne vinegar and extra-virgin olive oil and season with salt. Arrange the cucumbers, radishes, and mint on chilled salad plates. Dot the prepared tzatziki on the plates to finish.

Salad of Heirloom Tomatoes with Basil-Infused Mozzarella, Pickled Watermelon & Shallot Vinaigrette

(SERVES 6)

For the basil oil:

¼ cup salt
2 bunches fresh basil, stems removed
1 cup grapeseed oil

For the basil mozzarella:

2¼ teaspoons (one ¼ ounce package) powdered gelatin
⅛ cup whole milk
9 ounces fresh mozzarella
½ cup prepared basil oil
1 teaspoon Tabasco sauce
Salt to taste

For the pickled watermelon:

½ cup champagne vinegar or white wine vinegar
1 cup water
½ cup granulated sugar
1 pound seedless fresh watermelon, cut into 1- x 1- x 1-inch cubes

For the shallot vinaigrette:

¼ cup sherry wine vinegar
4 shallots, peeled and blanched until tender
½ cup extra-virgin olive oil
½ grapeseed or vegetable oil
Salt and white pepper to taste

For the salad:

5 multicolored heirloom tomatoes, washed and cut into ¼-inch slices
Salt and pepper to taste
Prepared shallot vinaigrette
Prepared basil mozzarella, cut into ¼-inch slices
Prepared pickled watermelon cubes
Micro-basil leaves

To make the basil oil, bring 1 gallon of water to a full boil in a medium stockpot. Add the salt and basil and cook for approximately 2 minutes. Remove the basil and place it immediately into a prepared ice bath. After the basil has cooled, remove it from the ice bath and squeeze it dry in a towel to remove any excess liquid. Combine the blanched basil and oil in a blender and mix on high speed to incorporate. Strain the basil oil through a coffee filter overnight, refrigerated.

To prepare the basil mozzarella, bloom the gelatin in the cold milk. When the gelatin is bloomed, heat the mixture until the gelatin is fully dissolved. In a food processor, combine the mozzarella, gelatin mixture, basil oil, and Tabasco. Process until combined and then season with salt to taste.

Pipe the mixture into synthetic sausage casings using a sausage press, if you have access to casings and a press. Alternately, lay plastic wrap on a work surface, pipe mozzarella onto plastic wrap laid on a work surface, and roll into a cylinder shape. Tie the ends and refrigerate until cool. Remove plastic wrap before slicing.

To make the pickled watermelon, combine the vinegar, water, and sugar in a small saucepan and bring to a full boil. When the sugar is completely dissolved, cool the mixture in the refrigerator. When the pickling liquid is cool, pour it over the watermelon and allow the fruit to marinate for at least 4 hours.

To make the vinaigrette, combine the vinegar and shallots in a blender and puree on high speed. Slowly drizzle in the oils until emulsified. Season to taste with the salt and pepper.

To prepare the salad, season the sliced tomatoes with salt, pepper, and some shallot vinaigrette. Arrange the tomatoes, mozzarella slices, and pickled watermelon on plates and garnish with micro-basil leaves. To finish, sauce the plates with the remaining shallot vinaigrette and basil oil to serve.

ST. HELENA

LOCAL FAVORITES

Considered the hourglass of the Napa Valley, as it connects the Spring and Howell Mountain appellations and bridges the towns of Calistoga and Yountville, St. Helena is surrounded by wineries that have been there from the beginning. This makes sense, as the town's first settlers—who named it for Mount St. Helena—discovered that the terroir of the region is perfectly suited for grape growing. The Beringer, Krug, and Christian Brothers names still echo through the valley as some of the earliest winemaking operations in the area. And the character of the town matches this venerated status.

Highway 29—also known as the St. Helena Highway—seems to narrow as you cross the town border, welcomed by tree-lined streets dotted with bakeries, bookstores, and trendy boutiques. Established early on as a vacationers' destination, St. Helena welcomed California's first hot springs resort in 1852, called White Sulphur Springs (now a private spiritual and yoga retreat). Over the years St. Helena has evolved into an even more stylish town, surrounded by countryside but populated with the elite in the food and wine world.

The famed Meadowood Resort and its gorgeous "Restaurant"—one of only two restaurants in the region that has three Michelin stars (the other being The French Laundry)—anchors St. Helena just off of the Silverado Trail. In town, Cindy Pawlcyn's newest restaurant, Brassica, welcomes food lovers nightly into its airy, Mediterranean-themed environment and Hiro Sone and Lissa Doumani's longstanding Michelin-starred Terra Restaurant (with newer addition Bar Terra) serves as a wine country icon. What many consider the first wine country establishment, Tra Vigne, formerly with Michael Chiarello at the helm, is now guided by chef Anthony "Nash" Cognetti and absolutely thriving. Its original terrace remains a popular gathering spot for locals and travelers alike, who enjoy a glass of California wine alongside cured meats and farmstead cheese at nearly any hour of the day. These powerhouses are joined by newer hot spots, such as Market and PRESS, showing that the revival of farm-fresh food is alive and well.

Brassica

641 Main Street
St. Helena, CA 94574
(707) 963-0700
www.brassicanapavalley.com
Chef/Owner: Cindy Pawlcyn

She owns several thousand cookbooks, filling two rooms at her home, and they span the globe in their focus on the world's cuisines and genres. From food philosophies, histories, and essays to specialty books on bread, sauces, cheese, Middle Eastern or French cuisine, "esoteric beverage books," the entire Richard Olney series from Time Life, or even eccentric treatises on "strange foods," chef Cindy Pawlcyn's collection is impressive—and beautifully explains her connection with food.

For Pawlcyn, celebrated chef and owner of several acclaimed Napa Valley restaurants—Mustards Grill, Cindy's Backstreet Kitchen, and her newest, Brassica Mediterranean Kitchen and Wine Bar—food is all about making people happy. And her interest in it began, simply, with a desire to delight her father.

"When I was a little kid, I'd help my mom cook because it was a way to make my dad presents," she explains, sharing how her siblings could play piano or draw, so she found her "own little niche" in the kitchen.

From these humble beginnings involving scratch breads and *galumpkis,* a classic butter-fried cabbage roll, Pawlcyn's repertoire gradually grew. She's cooked in Minneapolis, Chicago, San Francisco (where she opened the iconic Fog City Diner in an Airstream trailer), for thirty years in the Napa Valley, and even on TV—and her passion for learning about food has never waned. Her latest endeavor, Brassica—Latin for the genus of plants in the mustard family—is the perfect stage to spotlight her interest in Mediterranean cuisine.

With the prevalence of grapes throughout the Mediterranean region, Pawlcyn explains, "the foods grown there are all able to make dishes that are great with wine," making the focus a natural for a Napa Valley restaurant. Brassica's successfully wine-friendly food ranges from more familiar French, Italian, and Spanish classics to Moroccan, Tunisian, and Greek dishes that offer a chance to deliciously broaden diners' horizons. The super-simple starter of *bresaola,* an air-dried, salted beef that is an Italian style of charcuterie, served layered alternately with paper-thin slices of lemon and a drizzle of fresh herb oil, is a bracing, meaty, bright, light must. The sizzling grilled *haloumi* is delightful to both the tongue and the eye: Hot, chewy, and gooey at once, it arrives on the table in an adorable petite cast-iron pan. Brassica also offers an extensive and flexible wines-by-the-glass list and an intriguing "Brassica 12" category that features small local wineries who are friends of the restaurant—and none of which have tasting rooms. True to Pawlcyn's style, the entire dining experience, from the warm service to the food and wine, is unintimidating and inviting.

"I'm not a fancy cook, not an architectural cook, or a science cook," says Pawlcyn when describing her style—admitting it's easier to describe what she's not. "I like a lot of ingredients, and I like to have variety in my menus so they appeal to a broader audience. I'd rather have a busy little joint than a fancy little joint."

Baba Ghanoush

(SERVES 4)

1 pound eggplant, globe variety
1/8 cup tahini
1 garlic clove, minced
1/8 cup lemon juice
1/8 cup extra-virgin olive oil
Scant 1 teaspoon Aleppo pepper
½ teaspoon salt
¼ teaspoon black pepper
¼ teaspoon paprika
1/8 cup minced parsley
½ teaspoon ground cumin, toasted
4 pita bread rounds
Extra-virgin olive oil to taste
4 fresh, blanched grape leaves or lettuce leaves
1/8 teaspoon paprika
1 teaspoon sesame seeds, toasted
4 lemon wedges

Place the whole eggplants on the grill and roast until completely soft. Turn often and make sure the bottoms are soft. Grilling produces a smoky flavor. Alternatively, roast in a 400°F oven until completely soft.

Peel the eggplants and roughly chop the flesh. Place in a colander or sieve to drain the liquid out.

Combine the tahini, garlic, lemon juice, olive oil, Aleppo pepper, salt, black pepper, paprika, parsley, and cumin, mixing well. Add the drained eggplant and mix well.

Preheat oven to 350°F. Cut each pita round into 6–8 wedges. Brush each wedge lightly with olive oil and toast in the preheated oven for 10–15 minutes until crispy.

To serve, place a grape leaf or lettuce leaf on each plate and top with a scoop of baba ghanoush. Lightly sprinkle with paprika and toasted sesame seeds. Drizzle a small amount of extra-virgin olive oil on top. Place a lemon wedge to the side along with 5 wedges of toasted pita bread with the points facing out. (Serving 5 pita wedges per person will give you leftover wedges for those who want seconds.)

Farmstead Restaurant

738 Main Street
St. Helena, CA 94574
(707) 963-9181
www.longmeadowranch.com/Farmstead-Restaurant
Executive Chef: Stephen Barber

One of the best things about Farmstead Restaurant is what an absolute surprise it is once you get inside: It's a true southern, ranch-style gem sitting right in the thick of California wine country. And the casual passerby driving up Highway 29 would have no idea, but for the simple, bright Farmstead sign that sits amidst the gardens out front. So, that's pretty great—and so are the beans.

Chef Stephen Barber brings his Kentucky roots and love of good, simple food to Long Meadow Ranch Winery's relatively new restaurant, and it's a perfect pairing. Self-taught but extensively trained under some of the best American chefs—including John Currence of Mississippi's famed City Grocery and Norman Van Aiken of Miami's Norman's—Barber radiates quiet, southern charm and is defiant about the difference between grilling and barbecue: "People out here don't get it; they think 'barbecue' means outdoor grilling, but it's so much more." He's doing his best to educate the public: Barber and his team have done awe-inspiring outdoor, open-fire grilling—roasting whole animals on spits stuck into an ashy patch of ground adjacent to the restaurant.

"We're fortunate here in the Bay Area," Barber explains. "We can do whatever we feel we most want to do as chefs, and there's an audience for it," he says, describing the food-loving locals and tourists of the region and the incredible products. Sharing how the following week he planned to map out the restaurant's extensive garden for the next year: "We're going through the seed catalogue now. It's like Christmas!"

The "American farmhouse cooking" featured at Farmstead relies primarily on the produce, eggs, grass-fed beef, and olive oils produced right there on-site at Long Meadow Ranch. What they don't make themselves they get from local small producers.

Naturally, the ambience of the restaurant is very ranchy—friendly waitstaff all dressed in jeans and tucked-in plaid shirts, cattle-wrangling instruments dangling from the ceiling, and the smell of grilled meats and smoked foods emanating from the kitchen. In addition to its daily lunch and dinner service, Farmstead also does a "Tuesday Traditions" series, honoring Americana favorites such as chicken-fried steak and whole-smoked pig. Barber relishes the character of the restaurant and ranch, and loves being able to "stroll past the baby leeks out front" or serve beef raised right there on the farm—"it's a dream job for a chef." It also makes for a not-too-shabby down-home dining experience. Oh, and as for Barber's home-style smokehouse beans? Read on, and prepare to tuck in at home to an addictive ranch meal.

Cowboy Beans

(SERVES 4)

4 cups diced bacon, cut to ⅛ x ⅛ inch
1½ cups minced yellow onion
1 quart (4 cups) chicken stock
1½ cups pinquito beans
1 teaspoon dried oregano
1 teaspoon cumin
2 teaspoons chili powder
2 cups barbecue sauce, purchased (the chef couldn't divulge his secret sauce recipe; for purchased, he recommends Stubb's)
Kosher salt to taste

Heat the bottom of a medium sauce pot and sweat the bacon and onion for 5 minutes. Add the remaining ingredients with the exception of the barbecue sauce and salt, and allow the mixture to simmer on medium to low heat for 1 hour. Fold barbecue sauce into cooked beans and add salt to taste.

Braised Long Meadow Ranch Grass-Fed Beef Short-Rib with Creamy Polenta & Braised Spinach

(SERVES 4)

For the short ribs:

5 pounds short ribs
Salt and pepper to taste
2 cups all-purpose flour
2–3 tablespoons rice oil or olive oil, plus more as needed
1 recipe mirepoix (2 cups each diced carrots, onion, and celery)
2 tablespoons tomato paste
4 cups red wine
2 tablespoons unsalted butter

For the creamy polenta:

2 cups ground yellow cornmeal
7 cups chicken stock
1 cup heavy cream
2 teaspoons butter
Salt and white pepper to taste

For the braised spinach:

½ cup chicken stock
4 cups baby spinach
1 teaspoon unsalted butter
1 teaspoon chopped fresh thyme
Salt to taste

Preheat oven to 275°F.

Season ribs with salt and pepper, then coat with flour. In a medium saucepan over medium-high heat, brown ribs in oil and remove from the pan. Add mirepoix and cook until well caramelized. Add tomato paste and cook for 3–4 minutes. Deglaze with red wine and cook for another 3–4 minutes. Return ribs to the pan, cover, and braise in the preheated oven for 4 hours.

Carefully remove short ribs from braising liquid. Reduce braising liquid by half on medium heat. Puree the braising liquid in a blender with butter; serve over short ribs.

To make the polenta, heat cornmeal and stock in a medium saucepan over medium heat, stirring often for 15–20 minutes until thickened and tender. Finish on low heat with cream and butter. Check seasoning and adjust with salt and white pepper to taste.

To make the spinach, bring the stock to a boil in a small saucepot, fold in spinach, and cook for 5–10 minutes until tender. Finish with butter, thyme, and salt.

Grass-Fed Long Meadow Ranch Beef Meatballs with Caramelized Root Vegetables & Tomato Marmalade

(SERVES 4)

For the tomato marmalade:

4 cups whole peeled tomatoes, hand-crushed
1 small seedless orange, sliced thinly and slices quartered
½ seedless lemon, sliced thinly and slices quartered
4 cups white granulated sugar
1 teaspoon ground cinnamon
½ teaspoon ground cloves

For the caramelized root vegetables:

1 cup diced yellow onion
1 cup diced celery
1 cup diced carrot
Extra-virgin olive oil, as needed
Kosher salt

For the meatballs:

5 ounces (approximately 3 cups, loosely packed) torn white bread
1 cup whole milk
1½ pounds Long Meadow Ranch (or other favorite purveyor) grass-fed ground beef
½ cup grated grana cheese
1 tablespoon minced fresh rosemary
1 tablespoon minced fresh oregano
2 tablespoons chopped fresh parsley stems
1 teaspoon granulated garlic
1 teaspoon smoked paprika
1 tablespoon kosher salt
2 eggs, beaten

To make the tomato marmalade, mix all of the first set of ingredients together thoroughly. Cook over high heat to start in a medium saucepot, then reduce heat once the mixture boils. Boil and stir often until mixture reaches 225°F (check using a candy thermometer); this should take approximately 45 minutes to 1 hour.

To make the caramelized root vegetables, heat a medium skillet to 350°F and sauté the veggies for 5–10 minutes in a bit of olive oil with a pinch of salt until caramelized (golden brown), stirring often.

To make the meatballs, soak the bread in the milk for 30 minutes. Mix all the ingredients thoroughly and refrigerate for 1 hour.

Preheat oven to 500°F. Portion the meatball mixture as desired and cook in the preheated oven for 5–10 minutes to medium (or 4 minutes in a 750°F wood-burning oven). Garnish the meatballs with caramelized root veggies and tomato marmalade.

BERINGER VINEYARDS

2000 Main Street, St. Helena, CA 94574
(707) 967-4412 · www.beringer.com
Chief Winemaker: Laurie Hook

One of the earliest wineries in the Napa Valley—and the oldest continuously operating winery in the region—Beringer was founded in 1876 by brothers Jacob and Frederick Beringer, who may not have imagined what an institution it would grow to become. Jacob's former residence, the Hudson House, now serves as the winery's tasting salon and Culinary Arts Center. Frederick's mansion, the Rhine House, was named to the National Register of Historic Places in 2001.

Current chief winemaker Laurie Hook joined the Beringer team in 1986 as an enologist. About ten years later she was named assistant winemaker to wine master Ed Sbragia, and in 2000 she was promoted to chief. "The idea of doing something that connected me to the earth is what initially inspired me," Hook shares. "I soon realized that winemaking and, more specifically, drinking great wine brings people together."

She says the history and legacy of Beringer Vineyards has played a major role in her approach to winemaking.

"Making great wines is a balance of understanding your soils, working with the climate, and the variance of each vineyard," Hook explains. "But mostly, it is an intuitive process of taste, with minimal intrusions in that process. In essence, we are farmers looking to extract the best our fruit has to offer."

In other words, let the wine tell its own story. Walking the Beringer vineyards with Laurie, you begin to understand that story, as you sense the quiet confidence of the winemaker. She speaks fondly of her relationship with Sbragia, who as her mentor over the years, taught her about what to look for in the terroir and how to position the vineyard, but more importantly, how to respect the vineyard and bring out the true spirit of the fruit.

"It has given me the confidence to continue the legacy at Beringer that he was instrumental in developing."

On the subject of why white wines aren't typically aged like reds, Laurie says that white grape varietals are so appealing and the fruit has such vibrancy, a long aging won't enhance that. Some white wines are an exception, including Beringer's Nightingale, a late-harvest dessert wine that blends semillon with sauvignon blanc grapes.

Of Beringer's future, Hook says the winery's focus will be on more sustainability farming, moving toward more organic production. "The more you know your vineyard, the better your fruit," Hook says. She notes that there will always be variances in sun exposure, shade, and topography, but if you see and touch the vineyard, at the end of the day, you'll get better wine.

"It's about the fruit and the people," Hook says. "We're like a family at Beringer. And in each glass of wine lays the effort of a lot of great people."

Gott's Roadside

933 Main Street
St. Helena, CA 94574
(707) 963-3486
www.gotts.com
Proprietor: Joel Gott

If you didn't know he was an expert winemaker and local hamburger mogul, you might assume Joel Gott prefers to ride the waves on a surfboard. Casual, fun-seeking—even challenging his staff to a "crisp-off" in order to cunningly get more fantastic, freshly baked goods into the office—he has the air of a spirited teenager, but with adult expertise in running successful businesses.

And Gott's Roadside is exactly that.

The wildly popular hamburger joint began in the small, sophisticated town of St. Helena in 1949 as Taylor's Refresher, and Gott took over in 1999. Eventually converting its name—after expanding and personalizing its menu—Gott's Roadside now has two additional locations (in the Napa Oxbow Public Market and the San Francisco Ferry Building). It's easy to understand why.

The burgers are classic, incredibly juicy, and feature only the best ingredients. Gott's dices the fresh beef by hand, the proprietor explains, with extremely sharp knives—he says a dull knife leads to mashing of the meat and eventual shrinking when tossed on the grill. Their sweet potato fries are a fantastic complement, as are any of the shop's shake creations.

But Gott's has more than just burgers. Some devotees never stray from the fish tacos, which Gott says he designed after the popular version in Southern California. There's apparently also a secret menu, featuring special concoctions devised by staff members (the "Big and Tasty" involves fried chicken, bacon, and multiple styles of mayo).

What might be most surprising about the proprietor is his absolute connection to the vibe of the restaurant and the customers enjoying burgers picnic-style out back—on umbrella-adorned picnic tables Gott fashioned and built himself. As he sits among them, quietly observing, he notices an older couple and marvels at their apparent date lunch—fish tacos and Coronas, on a sunny day, at one of his handmade picnic tables.

"Look at them," Gott says. "They probably do that every week. I love it."

Grilled Ahi Burgers with Ginger-Wasabi Mayo

(SERVES 4)

For the Asian vinaigrette:

2 green onions
¼ cup rice wine vinegar
2 tablespoons sherry vinegar
3 tablespoons soy sauce
2 teaspoons hoisin sauce
2 teaspoons sambal sauce
1-inch piece fresh ginger, peeled and roughly chopped
2 tablespoons pickled ginger
2 teaspoons honey
2 tablespoons light sesame oil
2 tablespoons lime juice
¼ cup vegetable or peanut oil
1 garlic clove, roughly chopped
Red wine vinegar

For the slaw:

1 cup julienned Napa cabbage
½ cup julienned red cabbage
½ cup julienned carrots
¼ cup Asian vinaigrette

For the ginger-wasabi mayo:

1½ teaspoons wasabi powder
1 teaspoon water
1½ teaspoons lime juice
1 tablespoon chopped pickled ginger
½ cup mayonnaise

For ahi burgers:

4 (5-ounce) fresh ahi steaks, cut ½ inch thick
Soy sauce, for marinating
Oil, for brushing marinated ahi
4 burger buns

To make the vinaigrette, place all the ingredients in a blender and pulse to combine.

Toss the slaw ingredients with ¼ cup vinaigrette; reserve remainder of dressing for another use.

To make the mayo, mix wasabi powder with water and lime juice until it forms a paste, then whisk in pickled ginger and mayonnaise.

Build a hot charcoal fire or set gas grill on medium-high.

Place ahi steaks in a shallow pan with enough soy sauce to cover halfway. Marinate 2½ minutes, turn over the steaks, and marinate another 2½ minutes. Remove the steaks to a plate and brush lightly with oil.

Meanwhile, toast split buns and set aside on plates. Spread 1 tablespoon of ginger-wasabi mayo and ¼ cup of slaw on each bun surface.

Place ahi steaks over hot coals on the grill. After 45 seconds, turn 90 degrees to get some nice grill marks, wait 45 seconds more, then turn over and grill for 1 more minute.

Take ahi off the grill, place between dressed buns, and serve immediately.

Gott's Roadside Wisconsin Sourdough Burger

(SERVES 4)

For the barbecue sauce:

3 cups ketchup
½ cup dark brown sugar
⅓ cup distilled white vinegar
1½ tablespoons Worcestershire sauce
2 teaspoons yellow mustard
1½ tablespoons honey
2 teaspoons chili powder
1 teaspoon pepper
Pinch each of ginger, allspice, cayenne, and mace

For the burgers:

Melted butter, for toasting bread
8 slices fresh-baked sourdough bread
4 (⅓-pound) fresh coarse ground chuck (80 percent lean) burger patties (preferably Niman Ranch or another quality producer)
Salt and black pepper
8 slices thick-cut bacon
3 cup sliced mushrooms, sautéed in butter with salt and pepper to taste
4 slices cheddar cheese
½ cup mayonnaise (Best Foods or Hellman's preferred)
½ cup barbecue sauce

Mix together the barbecue sauce ingredients. The sauce will keep refrigerated for 2 weeks.

Prepare a medium-hot gas or charcoal grill.

Butter both sides of sourdough bread slices and place on cooler side of grill to toast, or toast separately in a cast-iron pan. Toast both sides to golden brown.

Meanwhile, place burgers on grill and salt and pepper generously. After 1½ minutes, turn burgers 90 degrees. After another 1½ minutes, flip the burgers over. Top them with warm bacon, then mushrooms, and cover with a slice of cheddar. Wait another 1½ minutes, then turn burgers 90 degrees. In the meantime, spread mayonnaise and barbecue sauce evenly over one side of every slice of toasted sourdough. When cheese is melted, place burgers on a slice of bread, top with another slice of bread, and serve!

Enjoy with your favorite beer or with a California cabernet, zinfandel, or Argentine malbec.

CHARBAY WINERY & DISTILLERY

4001 Spring Mountain Road, St. Helena, CA
(707) 963-9327 · www.charbay.com
Owners/Operators: Marko, Miles, and Susan Karakasevic

Known as "the still on the hill," Charbay Winery and Distillery was founded in 1983 by the Karakasevic family, but the family business of distilling actually goes back thirteen generations in Serbia, to the 1700s. This might explain why they're so good at it.

This Spring Mountain distillery was one of the first small-batch, artisanal distillers in California to create flavored vodkas. Today Charbay produces a handful of red and white wines as well as twelve different spirits, including whiskeys, brandies, ports, rum, and now tequila, but primarily focuses on seven distinct flavored vodkas, including a green tea aperitif. Blood orange–infused vodka and black walnut liqueur are the family's most widely sought libations. Take it from Marko, who began working for his father at age ten and is now the family's master distiller: The black walnut liqueur is "killer with a double espresso or drizzled on brownies."

Marko's passion is distilling whiskey, and he prefers to use Razor IPA, a local microbrew, as a base. "Quality beer means quality whiskey," he says, and given that whiskey is distilled from a mash of fermented grains—which is essentially beer—this sensible choice enables him to incorporate extra flavor from the start, aging the product in French oak barrels and compounding the hops. Charbay's excellent Double & Twisted label is distilled in the onion-shaped Charentais alembic pot still, a classic copper still the family considers best suited to produce superior spirits.

Charbay uses mostly local fruits for infusion and, like the chefs of the region, only buys the best products at the height of the season. They use high-elevation organic Meyer lemons and Oregon raspberries, along with the first-growth green tea from China for their unique aperitif.

Market

1347 Main Street
St. Helena, CA 94574
(707) 963-3799
www.marketsthelena.com
Chef/Owner: Eduardo Martinez
General Manager: Eddie Moore

Market restaurant, located in the heart of St. Helena, has a tasteful wine country ambience and local character that's not to be missed. The interior of the majestic stone building welcomes visitors with earthy tones, a stunning mahogany bar, and walls featuring local artwork, giving the space a cozy neighborhood feel and sense of authenticity.

The restaurant was originally opened in 2003 by Nick Peyton and Douglas Keane of the two-Michelin-star Cyrus restaurant in Healdsburg. Since its transition to the current team of general manager Eddie Moore and chef-owner Eduardo Martinez, the restaurant has not missed a beat.

Born in Mexico City, Martinez arrived in the Napa Valley in 1993 and worked in several stellar restaurants, including the Michelin-starred Auberge du Soleil and the Wine Spectator Greystone restaurant at The Culinary Institute of America. He says he fell in love with cooking and creating dishes in the kitchen of his mother, a great cook. He knew early on that he wanted to pursue cooking professionally and set off in pursuit of his dream, eventually connecting with Moore.

Moore, a political science major, arrived in the Napa Valley in 2004 with extensive restaurant experience—beginning with a job at Hydra in Cardiff-by-the-Sea, more than thirty years ago, and later at Purcell's Restaurant in Vail, Colorado. But it was at Michel Richard's famed Citronelle in Santa Barbara where he really honed and refined his skills and was inspired to follow a lifetime's passion to join great chefs, wineries, and restaurants in Napa.

Together, Martinez and Moore have created a restaurant that's a local favorite, with seasonally driven cuisine and a playful wine list featuring sought-after varietals from

a who's who of local vintners. Working with managing partner Roman Flores, the team's combined vision and commitment is to create a high-quality and memorable food and wine experience, using products sourced from organic farms.

Market has successfully created an atmosphere where people feel at home, crafting a balance of American-inspired comfort food with a strong emphasis on seasonal changes. And their commitment to the local community is evident, from the art on the walls to the delicious food on the plate.

Chopped Market Salad

(SERVES 4 AS A DINNER-SIZE SALAD)

For the whole-grain mustard vinaigrette:

¼ cup whole-grain mustard
¼ cup Dijon mustard
3 tablespoons red wine vinegar
2 tablespoons sherry vinegar
¾ cup extra-virgin olive oil
Salt and pepper to taste

For the salad:

1 bunch broccoli, broken into small florets
4 jumbo orange carrots, diced
1 whole head cauliflower, broken into small florets
¼ head iceberg lettuce
¼ cup sweet cherry tomatoes
¼ cup sweet white corn kernels
1 avocado, peeled and diced
3 hard-boiled eggs, finely diced
5 tablespoons cooked and crumbled Hobbs' bacon (or other good-quality bacon)
5 tablespoons Point Reyes blue cheese (or other favorite blue cheese)
Salt and pepper to taste

To make the vinaigrette, combine all the ingredients except the olive oil in a Cuisinart or blender. Add olive oil slowly while continuing to mix. Adjust texture with water to provide desired consistency. Add salt and pepper to taste.

Blanch broccoli, carrots, and cauliflower in salted boiling water until al dente (slightly undercooked). Cool in an ice-water bath, drain, and let dry.

Dice the iceberg lettuce into ¼-inch sections and put into a salad bowl with chilled, blanched vegetables. Add tomato, corn, avocado, hard-boiled eggs, bacon, and blue cheese. Toss all ingredients together and add mustard vinaigrette. Season with salt and pepper and enjoy!

Very Adult Mac n' Cheese

(SERVES 4 AS AN ENTREE OR 6–8 AS AN APPETIZER)

1 pound elbow macaroni
2 tablespoons extra-virgin olive oil
1 cup sour cream
3 tablespoons Dijon mustard
1 cup panko (Japanese-style bread crumbs), toasted
3 cups heavy cream
1 cup grated Fiscalini sharp white cheddar cheese
(or any other artisanal sharp)
¼ cup grated Parmigiano-Reggiano
(or other Parmesan)
½ cup cooked and crumbled Hobbs' bacon
(or other good-quality bacon)
3 tablespoons chopped chives
3 tablespoons chopped parsley
Salt and pepper to taste

Cook elbow macaroni according to package instructions, but shorten the cooking time slightly so the noodles are al dente (slightly undercooked). Drain the macaroni, toss with olive oil, and allow noodles to cool on a cookie sheet. Once the noodles are at room temperature, toss them with the sour cream and Dijon mustard.

Meanwhile, preheat oven to 275°F. Toast the bread crumbs by spreading them on a cookie sheet and bake in the preheated oven until they are golden brown. This should take approximately 8–10 minutes, but check often to avoid burning. Set aside to cool to room temperature.

To finish the dish, heat heavy cream in a medium stockpot over medium-high heat until hot but not boiling. Add grated cheddar and Parmesan cheeses. Stir until cheese has melted and has incorporated into the cream. Add the macaroni and crumbled bacon and stir to combine. Once the noodles are heated thoroughly, stir in the chives and parsley. Season with salt and pepper to taste.

Pour into a large serving dish or 4 individual bowls and garnish with a heavy sprinkling of the toasted bread crumbs.

PRESS

587 St. Helena Highway
St. Helena, CA 94574
(707) 967-0550
www.pressSthelena.com
Owner: Leslie Rudd
Executive Chef: Stephen Rogers
General Manager: Allison Yoder

When it comes to being a restaurant in wine country, PRESS takes that distinction seriously. You can't help but think about wine when visiting this elegant, ultra-comfortable St. Helena steak house—it's even named for the pressing of grapes that leads to the most famous product of the region.

PRESS describes its wine program as "a celebration of the heritage and history of Napa Valley" and boasts more than 1,000 local wines, dating back to the 1950s, to prove it. This commitment reflects owner Leslie Rudd's (also a winemaker and owner of the adjacent gourmet food emporium, Dean & Deluca) passion for the region. Expert sommeliers Kelli White and Scott Brenner know their stuff and recommend pairings to highlight both the wine and the food. The restaurant's gorgeous design elements—including a high wood-beamed farm ceiling, two giant fireplaces, and a beautiful bar made of a single, long piece of black walnut wood from North Carolina—draw in the diner.

But to understand PRESS, one must go beyond the wine and the incredible space. General manager Allison Yoder and executive chef Stephen Rogers are charming in a way that makes one immediately understand the personality of the restaurant. Yoder, an opera singer, and Rogers, a classical pianist and vocal coach, met and fell in love in Philadelphia, and never did they imagine that they would one day be running a restaurant in California's wine country. But eighteen years (and twin boys) later, after stints in New York and Florida, that is just where they are, and loving it.

They are relaxed and connected—to each other, their customers, and the food. And their energy seems to infuse the restaurant with an organic, artistic charm. "Music, art, food—it's all about creativity," Rogers says. Yoder agrees, saying the "rush" you get on stage is similar to the feeling at the end of the night at the restaurant.

Though both have worked in restaurants since they were teens, supplementing their musician incomes, Rogers only recently joined the back of the house as chef, where he "feels at home." Inspired by what the gardener for the burgeoning space out back grows at any given moment, Rogers develops specials to showcase the season—his incredible take on a Greek salad is completely garden-driven. But he also turns out countless perfectly grilled steaks, cooked over cherry and almond wood, paired with the best comfort food classics (think truffle mac and cheese and a crispy-soft potato cake to haunt your dreams) each night.

PRESS offers exactly what you want in a steak house experience: a warm welcome, a relaxed atmosphere, supremely delicious comfort foods, and fantastic wines—most of which were made within thirty miles of your cozy booth.

PRESS Brussels Sprouts

(SERVES 2–4 AS A SIDE DISH)

3- to 4-ounce slab bacon,
cut into ½-inch cubes (lardons)
20–24 small brussels sprouts (about 1 pound)
¼ cup melted duck fat (or canola oil)
Salt and pepper to taste

Render the bacon in a sauté pan over medium-low heat until most of the fat has rendered off and the bacon is brown and crispy (about 8–10 minutes). Set bacon aside.

Preheat oven to 450°F.

Wash and clean the brussels sprouts. Trim the stem end and remove any rough outer leaves. Cut in half from the stem end to top.

In a large sauté pan or skillet, add the melted duck fat or oil and place all of the brussels sprouts flat-side down in a single layer. Place over medium-high heat and sauté until the brussels sprouts begin to lightly brown on the bottom. Season with salt and pepper and add the bacon lardons.

Move the pan to the preheated oven and continue roasting the brussels sprouts for about 3 minutes. Give the brussels sprouts a good toss, then place back in the oven until cooked through (another 2–3 minutes).

Hiramasa Tartare

(SERVES 4)

For the tartare:

½ pound hiramasa, diced (or hamachi or sushi-grade tuna)
½ cup diced mango
1 teaspoon finely minced red onion
1 teaspoon finely minced red chili
1 teaspoon peeled, seeded, and finely minced cucumber
½ teaspoon finely minced pickled ginger
½ teaspoon finely chopped fresh cilantro
Pinch of salt

For the sesame-lime vinaigrette:

1 tablespoon freshly squeezed lime juice
3 tablespoons grapeseed or canola oil
½ teaspoon toasted sesame oil
Pinch of salt
Pinch of sugar

For the wasabi emulsion:

2 tablespoons mayonnaise or homemade aioli
1 teaspoon wasabi paste
2 leaves fresh basil, finely chopped
2 leaves fresh mint, finely chopped
Freshly squeezed lime juice
Pinch of salt

To serve:

Salt and pepper to taste
Optional: ½–1 cup lotus root chips or other root vegetable chips to serve (available in specialty markets)

Combine all the ingredients for the tartare and set aside.

With a whisk, combine all the ingredients for the sesame-lime vinaigrette and set aside.

Using a hand-held immersion blender or a whisk and a strong arm, combine all the ingredients for the wasabi emulsion and set aside.

To serve, combine the tartare with the sesame-lime vinaigrette and season to taste with salt and pepper. Top with a few crispy lotus root chips, or other root vegetable chips, and garnish plate with the wasabi emulsion.

TERRA

1345 Railroad Avenue
St. Helena, CA 94574
(707) 963-8931
www.terrarestaurant.com
Chefs/Owners: Hiro Sone and Lissa Doumani

She is of Lebanese descent, and he, Japanese. She grew up in a restaurant family in Los Angeles (which evolved into a winemaking family in the Napa Valley), and he was raised in a family of rice farmers in rural Japan. They met almost thirty years ago while working for Wolfgang Puck in the heyday of his burgeoning culinary empire, and through the language of the kitchen—and letters across continents—they fell in love.

Lissa Doumani and Hiro Sone are the powerhouse pastry chef/chef team behind Terra Restaurant and the adjacent Bar Terra in St. Helena. They bring extraordinary culinary talent to the chic wine country town (as well as to nearby San Francisco, where their newest restaurant, Ame, is located), along with a fantastic rapport with each other. They often disagree, Doumani says, but productively. And they have a lot of fun.

Every Halloween they invite Terra customers to dress up—and do so themselves. They travel frequently, eat out regularly, and comically share stories about visiting Sone's still-rural family in Japan and all the cultural differences that are still viscerally apparent. Their food tastes are both distinct and convergent: Sone is up for the Vietnamese noodle dish pho at any time of the day, when they're traveling or in "the city" of San Francisco, while Doumani often prefers a more proper sit-down dinner. But they love each other's food as well, and bring their sensibilities together in an amazing way at Terra.

The restaurant has been Michelin-starred for many years running, and for good reason. A blend of the duo's global influences—including their own backgrounds as well as the colorful, distinctive cuisines of their travels—it is not sufficient to call it fusion. Now almost twenty-five years old, Terra offers a flexible prix-fixe menu nightly: You may choose four, five, or six courses from a slate of delicious options, including dishes that combine Japanese, Mexican, and French influences seamlessly (effortlessly pairing a scallop with tripe stew seems like, perhaps, something only they can do). Desserts, ever important at the restaurant with a "Pastry Princess" (Doumani's nickname) at the helm, range from comforting seasonal tarts with house-made ice cream to very elegant dishes such as a fromage blanc cheesecake, with lemon sablé and cabernet berry compote.

Ever a wine country icon, but always evolving, this super-couple chef team's Terra is certain to persist long beyond its quarter-century mark, continuing to offer a delicious dining experience that is both of the earth and like a letter from abroad.

Sautéed Forest Mushrooms with Slow-Cooked Jidori Egg

(SERVES 4)

This is a great dish for the fall when local mushrooms abound. It is also a very easy dish to prepare for friends. The bread and slow-cooked eggs can all be done ahead. When eating this dish, tell your guests to break the egg and mix it into the mushrooms. The combination of the richness from the yolk and the mushrooms is sensuous, and the crunch of the toast brings it all together.

For the chicken stock:

Chef's note: Make the day before.

¼ cup vegetable oil
2 chicken carcasses, cut into 2-inch pieces
Water
¼ cup thinly sliced carrots
½ cup thinly sliced yellow onions
1 garlic clove, smashed
1 tablespoon tomato paste
1 fresh thyme sprig
1 bay leaf

For the jidori egg:

¼ baguette, a piece approximately 4 inches long
4 jidori eggs (free-range chicken eggs)
4 tablespoons butter
2 tablespoons chopped shallots
Pinch of minced garlic
1 tablespoon julienned pancetta (cut into small matchsticks)
3 cups forest mushrooms such as chanterelle, porcini, hedgehog, black trumpet, matsutake, maitake, or morel, cleaned, well dried, and cut into bite-size pieces
⅛ teaspoon freshly chopped thyme
Salt and freshly ground pepper to taste
⅔ cup chicken stock
1 teaspoon chopped parsley

To make the chicken stock, heat oil in a large sauté pan over high heat, add carcasses, and sauté until golden brown, using a wooden spatula to scrape the bottom of the pan to keep the carcasses from getting too dark. Transfer the carcasses to a large stock pot and add water to cover. Bring to a boil over high heat, then reduce to a simmer.

Meanwhile, into the sauté pan you just used, add carrots, onions, and garlic and cook until the vegetables are caramelized. If necessary, add a little more oil, then add tomato paste to the pan and keep stirring and scraping with a wooden spatula. Cook until the tomato paste becomes light brown in color. Add about 1 cup water to the pan, bring to a boil, and scrape the bottom of the pan to get brown bits into the liquid.

Pour the contents of the sauté pan into the stock pot. Bring to a boil again, then reduce to a simmer and skim all impurities that come up to the surface. Add thyme and bay leaf and simmer for 1 hour. If necessary, add boiling water to keep the carcasses covered with water.

Strain through a fine-mesh sieve into a medium pot, return to the stove, and at a simmer reduce to ⅔ cup. Cool, cover, and refrigerate.

The next day there will be a layer of fat on the top of the stock that has become solid. With a large spoon, carefully scoop it off and discard. Cover the stock and refrigerate until use.

Preheat oven to 350°F. Slice the baguette diagonally to ⅛ inch thick. Place the slices on a cookie sheet in a single layer and bake in the preheated oven until golden brown. After removing from the oven, sprinkle with a little salt and set aside to cool. Once cooled, you can store the croutons in an airtight container to use later if you like.

Place the eggs in a small bowl and cover with room-temperature water for 15 minutes to temper. Meanwhile, in a medium saucepot, bring 4 inches of water to 146°F.

Gently place the eggs into the water and stir gently in a circular motion to keep the eggs moving (this process will help keep the yolks in the center of the white). At the same time, bring the water back to 146°F and keep stirring for about 5 minutes. Monitor the temperature so it stays at 146°F for 30 minutes. Remove the eggs from the water and keep in a warm place until the mushrooms are ready. (If you are going to use the eggs later in the day or the next day, refrigerate until 1 hour before you are ready to use them. Remove from the refrigerator and let stand at room temperature for 1 hour, then place in a bowl of hot tap water for 15 minutes to warm.)

In a large sauté pan, melt the butter over medium heat. Add the shallots, garlic, and pancetta and cook for about 3 minutes or until the vegetables are tender. Increase the heat to high, add the mushrooms and thyme, and stir. Season with salt and pepper and cook until the surface of the mushrooms is caramelized, then add the stock and reduce by two-thirds. Stir in the parsley.

Divide the mushrooms and sauce among 4 warm dinner bowls and make a little dent in the center of the mushrooms for the egg. Carefully crack eggs and place in the middle of the mushrooms. Arrange the croutons around the egg and serve.

Panzanella with Local Goat Cheese

(SERVES 4)

Panzanella is a classic Tuscan tomato and bread salad and is our favorite dish during the long summers in the Napa Valley. The most important ingredient is the tomatoes. They should be the best you can buy, vine-ripened and bursting with flavor. Try to mix and match varieties—you can go wild with different sizes, colors, and acidity. Instead of the goat cheese you can try Parmesan cheese or Burrata cheese.

For the vinaigrette:

½ cup extra-virgin olive oil
1 tablespoon sherry wine vinegar
1 tablespoon capers
1½ teaspoons chopped anchovy
¼ teaspoon chopped garlic
Salt to taste

For the panzanella:

Baguette, enough for 1½ cups of croutons
1 garlic clove, peeled
3 cups diced vine-ripened tomatoes, in 1-inch squares
1 Japanese cucumber (or ½ hothouse cucumber), quartered lengthwise then cut crosswise into ½-inch pieces
¼ cup thinly sliced red onion
2 teaspoons chopped fresh basil
Salt and freshly ground pepper
12 kalamata olives
12 yellow pear tomatoes or Sweet 100 tomatoes
½ cup crumbled goat cheese
2 tablespoons extra-virgin olive oil
4 fresh basil sprigs

To make the vinaigrette, combine all the ingredients in a blender and puree 1 minute. Season with salt. Set aside.

Preheat oven to 500°F. Slice the baguette in half lengthwise. Rub all over with the garlic, then cut in half again lengthwise. Cut these strips into ¾-inch cubes. Bake on a cookie sheet, crust-side down, until golden brown and crispy but still soft inside, about 3 minutes; watch carefully. Let cool.

To make the panzanella, combine the vine-ripened tomatoes, cucumber, onion, basil, toasted bread, and vinaigrette in a large bowl. Toss well. Season with salt and pepper.

Divide the panzanella among 4 bowls or plates. Garnish each portion with 3 olives and 3 pear tomatoes. Top with crumbled goat cheese and drizzle with extra-virgin olive oil. Garnish with a basil sprig.

Tra Vigne

1050 Charter Oak Avenue
St. Helena, CA 94574
(707) 963-4444
www.travignerestaurant.com
Chef: Anthony "Nash" Cognetti

In Italian, *tra vigne* means "among the vines." It's hard to get more wine country than that. Originally opened in 1986 by chef, television host, and now head of a culinary-brand empire, Michael Chiarello, the restaurant was one of the first in the Napa Valley to really represent the region. And it's still around, under new ownership—and just as, if not more, delicious as before.

For the last six years, chef Anthony "Nash" Cognetti has been at the helm, and brings every bit of himself to bear in the restaurant. A native of Scranton, Pennsylvania, Cognetti was first exposed to food by his family's produce business. He later attended the University of Vermont in Burlington for his undergraduate degree in business management, working in kitchens to help pay his bills. But after graduation, he wanted something more—so he sold everything but his cookbooks and trekked across country to the Golden State.

He enrolled at the California Culinary Academy in San Francisco, after which his culinary résumé soared, with positions at various city restaurants, including the acclaimed PlumpJack Cafe. Driven by a yearning for more sun and a slower pace of life, Cognetti accepted a sous chef job at Tra Vigne, stayed for a bit, then went to Italy, where he worked for a two-Michelin-star restaurant. The experience was intensely influential on the young chef. He is now a devotee of the Italian approach to food—simplicity, big bold flavors, and perfect seasonal ingredients.

While some Italian preparations feel too simple for California expectations, Cognetti says, some of what you get at his Napa Valley restaurant is just as you would have it in the mother country: "The rigatoni alla carbonara [recipe featured] is exactly how I was taught to do it in Italy." And that food, pretty much all of it, is kind of amazing.

The Tra Vigne team makes a unique mozzarella *al minuto*—hand-stretched to order—that will make you think you've never tasted mozzarella before. (Cognetti had ultra-fresh mozzarella in Italy, and so loved its "seepy" quality that he "pays someone to pull the stuff to order, all day long.") And with incredible pizzas alongside all the house-made pastas—from an earthy, comforting rabbit ragu-dressed sage pappardelle to the lightest, pillowy fresh ricotta-stuffed agnolotti with summer squash—no choice will lead you astray, especially when paired with any number of the fabulous, mostly local wines on offer.

Reflecting on the restaurant's longtime status in the area, Cognetti says proudly, "Tra Vigne was here before the Napa Valley was a food and wine mecca. The restaurant's first clients were grape farmers—and locals are still our most important clientele. [In twenty-five years] I hope we continue to be rooted in old-school, fundamental Italian cuisine, but also still on the cutting edge of new-school American food trends. No molecular gastronomy."

And Cognetti just may still be there then. A true fixture at the restaurant, he's not interested in the modern trappings of TV shows and media omnipresence that seem to

go with the job of a chef today. "I'm always here—because I like it. I like being here with my team, cooking, being part of the restaurant."

His best advice for the home cook? "The whole point of Italian cuisine is to highlight great ingredients, so don't skimp. It's less about what you put into a dish and more about what you don't." The bottom line: Don't make corn soup when it's not corn season.

Wood Oven-Roasted Dungeness Crab with Balsamic-Marinated Cippolini Onions & Mâche

(SERVES 4)

For the crab:

Salt to taste
1 teaspoon chili flakes
2 cups dry white wine
4 Meyer lemons
4 (1½- to 2-pound) live Dungeness crabs
2 tablespoons chopped fresh garlic
3 tablespoons extra-virgin olive oil
2 teaspoons chopped calabrian chilies
1 cup Meyer lemon juice
¼ cup sweet butter

For the aioli:

2 whole eggs
1 garlic clove, peeled and finely chopped
2 teaspoon Dijon mustard
⅛ cup crab juice from previous step, strained again through a fine skimmer
1 Meyer lemon, zested and juiced
2 cups olive oil

For the balsamic onions:

6 tablespoons sweet butter
¼ cup brown sugar
2 pounds cippolini onions, peeled and left whole
1 bunch fresh thyme, picked and chopped
3 cups balsamic vinegar

8 cups mâche (or watercress, if mâche is unavailable), washed
French bread to serve

Bring a large pot of water able to easily accommodate the crabs to a rolling boil. Season with salt, then add the chili flakes and white wine. Slice the lemons in half and add to the pot as well. Using a sturdy pair of tongs, add the crabs to the pot and cook for approximately 4 minutes per pound. Remove from the liquid and place on a baking tray to cool at room temperature. Discard the remaining cooking liquid.

Meanwhile, sauté the garlic in the olive oil over medium heat until cooked but not browning at all. Add the calabrian chilies and remove from the heat.

Once the crabs are cool enough to handle, remove the body shell and set aside for later use. Drain all of the crab juices into a bowl and strain through a mesh skimmer. In a small saucepan, bring the juice to a simmer and reduce by half. Strain the crab juice again and set aside to cool in the refrigerator. It will be used for the aioli later on.

Crack the legs off the crabs and separate the body into 4 pieces. Using the back of a heavy chef's knife or a crab mallet, crack the legs gently until the shell just breaks. Arrange the crabs in a large roasting pan and add half of the lemon juice and a copious drizzle of extra-virgin olive oil. Slide into the oven and bake for 4–5 minutes. (If using a grill, toss the crab in the olive oil and half of the lemon juice, then place directly onto the grill and cook until charred. Remove and place in a roasting pan, coat with the garlic and chilies, add the butter and lemon juice, and then continue to cook in the pan for the remaining time.)

Remove the crabs from the oven and add the garlic-chili mix, the rest of the lemon juice, and the butter. Toss the crab pieces around to coat and cook for 4–5 minutes more.

To make the aioli, combine the eggs, garlic, mustard, crab juice, and lemon zest in a mixing bowl or food processor. Slowly whisk in the oil to form an emulsification. Whisk in the lemon juice and season with salt to taste.

To make the onions, melt the butter and brown sugar in a large sauté pan or brazier. Cook until the sugar is bubbling and beginning to caramelize. Add the onions and the thyme and stir to coat and combine. Reduce the heat and cook for 10–12 minutes, being careful not to burn the sugar around the edges. If the pan gets too hot, add a splash of water and continue on. Add the vinegar and increase the heat to high. Cook 8–10 minutes more, stirring frequently, until the vinegar is reduced and begins to coat the onions. Remove from heat and set aside.

To assemble, arrange a bit of balsamic onions on each plate. Attempt to "re-create" the original shape of the crab by placing body pieces in the middle, surrounded by the legs with the claws in front. Drizzle generously with the aioli. Place the body shell on top of each "crab," leaving the legs and claws sticking out. Dress a bit of mâche with a squeeze of Meyer lemon and olive oil and arrange around the crabs (portion 2 cups of mâche per person). Garnish with Meyer lemon wedges and serve with toasted buttery French bread.

Classic Roman-Style Rigatoni alla Carbonara

(SERVES 4)

Legend has it that the word *carbonara* is derived from the miners outside of Rome who enjoyed a hearty pasta made with cured pork jowels, fresh eggs, and Pecorino Romano cheese. They would adorn the dish with copious amounts of black pepper, which was reminiscent of the specks of carbon that covered their hands and clothing after a day in the mines. The true Roman carbonara is made with guanciale bacon that is cured from pork jowels as opposed to pancetta or American bacon, which comes from the belly. The classic version contains no cream whatsoever, and the creamy sauce is actually made from a liaison of pasta water, fresh eggs, Parmesan cheese, and the rendered fat from the guanciale. Add fresh spring peas to the dish only when in season, between May and June.

1 pound rigatoni pasta
2 cups diced guanciale bacon
1 cup thinly sliced yellow onion
4 whole eggs
4 egg yolks
1 cup blanched fresh peas (optional)
Kosher salt to taste
¼ cup grated Parmesan cheese
Cracked black pepper to taste
¼ cup shaved Pecorino Romano cheese

In a 10- to 12-quart stockpot, bring water to a boil with a copious amount of salt. Add the rigatoni and stir briefly.

Render the bacon in a large sauté pan or brazier until very crispy. Using a slotted spoon, remove the crispy bacon from the pan and reserve. Add the sliced onions to the pan and sauté in the remaining bacon fat until translucent.

Meanwhile, whisk the whole eggs and egg yolks together until light and frothy.

When rigatoni is cooked just al dente, reserve a cup of pasta water and set aside. Then add the drained rigatoni along with the reserved bacon to the pan. If using fresh peas, add them at this point as well. Season with salt and stir to combine. Remove from the heat and stir in the Parmesan cheese and eggs. Season the pasta vigorously with freshly cracked black pepper.

Return the pan to low heat and add a couple ladles of the pasta water to temper the eggs. Cook slowly while continuously stirring until a creamy sauce is formed. Be careful not to overheat at the risk of scrambling the eggs and breaking the sauce. Serve topped with shaved Pecorino Romano cheese.

DUCKHORN VINEYARDS

1000 Lodi Lane, St. Helena, CA 94574
(888) 354-8885 · www.duckhorn.com
Chairman: Dan Duckhorn; Executive Winemaker: Bill Nancarrow

Duckhorn Vineyards is centered on Marlee's vineyard, named for the wife of Dan Duckhorn, chairman of the board, and the first estate ever planted by the winery. The chairman continues to give the winery team a historical perspective, remaining intimately involved in long-term strategies, while Bill Nancarrow, executive winemaker, produces superb wines on a daily basis at this charming winery near St. Helena.

In 2003 New Zealand–born Nancarrow was handpicked by the Duckhorn family and became only the third winemaker at the winery, situated in what he calls "an ideal climate for making red wines." The land around the original estate contains rich, heavy soil that produces great sauvignon blanc and semillon varietals. And Patzimaro, Duckhorn's showcase in St. Helena, is a vineyard designate producing great cabernet sauvignon and cabernet franc. It is named as a tribute to the Hitaro family who works the vineyard, for their village in Mexico. Wines from the Patzimaro vineyard reflect its olive notes and are complex and intense, lending themselves to pairing well with meat dishes.

A bit north of St. Helena, Duckhorn's Three Palms vineyard produced one of the winery's first vintages in 1978—a stunning merlot that put Duckhorn on the map. This wine's terroir is part of the old wash of Selby Creek on the southern boundary of the vineyard, full of small river stones. The land is free-draining and very warm, which seems counterintuitive in winemaking because you don't want to cook out the fruit, but here the grapes are superior and have great concentration.

Glassware plays a significant role in the wine experience, and with so many choices, Nancarrow explains its evolution in design. Riedel glassware has influenced taste, he says, by creating varied shapes and sizes using fine crystal. Narrower glasses are meant to retain the aromatic characteristics of lighter, brighter varietals such as sauvignon blanc, Riesling, and zinfandel—generating a more direct flavor profile and, in turn, adding to the inherent intensity of the wines. On the other hand, varietals like chardonnay and pinot noir benefit from a larger opening in the glass, which opens the aromas and contributes to a richer and more well-rounded character.

The design of the rim also plays a significant role in the drinker's experience with the wine, as it is solely responsible for how the wine is directed onto your palate, or more specifically, the tongue. If the rim is wide, the wine will run across your palate, generating a smooth mouth feel and enhancing the fullness of the wine. A narrower rim will direct the wine down the center of the tongue, creating a more direct intensity.

Wine Spectator Greystone at the CIA

2555 Main Street
St. Helena, CA 94574
(707) 967-1010
www.ciachef.edu/restaurants/wsgr
Chef Instructor: Lars Kronmark
Executive Chef: Almir Da Fonseca

To really understand the culinary picture of Northern California's wine country, one must visit the St. Helena campus of The Culinary Institute of America. Many of the region's (and the country's) chefs have studied here, the beautiful stone building was once home to the renowned Christian Brothers winery, and the campus functions not only as a revered space for culinary education but also as a multipurpose culinary destination—with classes for food and wine enthusiasts, a great retail space, and a fantastic restaurant.

Learning is a theme that infuses all aspects of the venerated establishment, whether it be at its "flavor bar" (learning about varieties of chocolate), on a stroll through the Vintners Hall of Fame in the impressive barrel room, or enjoying flights of wine or olive oil, replete with a mini-lesson from the server, at the restaurant. The school's annual global conference, "Worlds of Flavor," offers a chance for in-depth learning about the cuisine of a specific country and draws culinary stars the world over (Ferran Adria participated in the Spain-focused event). Not to forget its placement in wine country, the school's new partnership with the Napa Valley Vintners Association offers weekly small gatherings with a local vintner, for more casual learning about the story behind the wine.

Former director of education, Adam Busby, says of the Napa Valley, "For a foodie, there are so many things at your fingertips and you don't have to do very much to make them taste good. It's why I moved here: It's the epicenter of food and wine in North America. But more than that—the classroom is the valley that surrounds us. If you're into food and wine, it's the place to be."

Going beyond the incredible produce on hand, the quality of breads and diversity of cheeses available in the region is unparalleled anywhere else in North America, Busby says. But he is quick to point out that the students are the heart of the place. They run everything at the campus—from the production gardens and the signature "seven terraces of organic culinary herbs" to the restaurant and all of the educational experiences contained within.

Chef/instructor Lars Kronmark, who also lives locally, grows cabernet franc grapes, and makes his own wine, has been with the school since the beginning. He says the CIA's mark on the culinary landscape of the country is pervasive. Even if you never get a chance to visit the CIA, Kronmark assures you that you likely already have a connection to it: "Most people know somebody who went here. With 40,000 alumni, I guarantee you, there's a restaurant in your town with a CIA alumni."

Learning truly does dictate all at the CIA, as Kronmark had to dash off at the end of the interview to return to his seminar on heritage pigs—seventy-five students awaited.

Sweet White Corn Soup with Crab & Chive Oil

(SERVES 6)

The first appearance of local sweet corn is the inspiration for this heavenly soup. This one should have you seeking picked-that-morning corn from your farmers' market or a nearby farm stand. Layers of interest are created by complementary tastes (that of the corn and the crab) and those flavors that act as contrasts (the sweetness of the corn and the smokiness of the bacon). The herbal undertones suggest the verdant qualities of the garden and the lightness that is life in the wine country in late summer. If you can find an off-dry sparkling wine, it should keep up with the sweetness of the corn and add an attractive texture to the creamy soup.

For the chive oil (yields about 1 cup):

***Chef's note:** Easy to make and the essence of summer, chive oil can also be used on tomato salads, grilled fish, over niçoise olives, and on couscous and other grain salads. The oil can be kept in the refrigerator for one week.*

2 bunches chives (about 1 ounce each)
1 cup olive oil
¼ teaspoon salt, or as needed

For the soup:

6 ears sweet corn (about 12 to 16 ounces each)
2 ounces applewood-smoked slab bacon, cut into thirds (about 2-inch pieces)
2 tablespoons butter
2 small yellow onions (about 8 to 10 ounces each), peeled and sliced
10 fresh thyme sprigs
1 fresh sage sprig
2 quarts (8 cups) chicken stock
1½ pounds Yukon Gold potatoes, peeled and sliced
1 teaspoon kosher salt, or to taste
½ teaspoon freshly ground black pepper, or as needed
¾ cup heavy cream
4 ounces Maine, rock, or peekytoe crabmeat or lobster meat
6 tablespoons chive oil

To make the chive oil, place the chives, olive oil, and salt in a blender. Puree until smooth, about 30 seconds. Let sit overnight covered in a stainless steel bowl. Strain the puree through a fine-mesh sieve and store in a plastic squeeze bottle or small container in the refrigerator.

Cut the kernels from the cobs. Reserve the kernels and 2 corncobs.

Place the bacon in a large heavy-bottomed soup pot over low heat and cook until the fat is rendered, about 4 minutes. Do not brown the bacon.

Add the butter and onions to the pot and sweat until soft and translucent over medium-high heat, about 4–5 minutes. Tie together the thyme and sage sprigs and add to the onion mixture.

Add the chicken stock, potatoes, and corncobs to the pot. Bring to a simmer over medium heat, season with salt and pepper, and simmer until the potatoes are cooked through, about 30 minutes. Add the cream and bring the soup to a boil. Reduce to a simmer, add the reserved kernels, and simmer for 5 minutes.

Remove the soup from the heat and discard the bacon, corncobs, and herbs. Blend the soup until smooth, about 1–2 minutes. Pass the soup through a fine-mesh sieve into a saucepan and adjust seasonings. Gently reheat soup.

Divide soup into 6 soup bowls. Garnish each bowl with about 2 tablespoons crab and 1 tablespoon or so of chive oil. Serve immediately.

NAPA

MAINS & SIDES

It has both a river and a train. Its character had become a bit sleepy through its late twentieth-century transition from a town of industrial activity—including tanneries and prune processing—to one of hospitality and wine tourism. But it is sleepy no more, possibly due to the youthful quality of its demography—the median age of the population is about thirty-six—though more likely due to the thriving restaurant and winemaking scene shaping the town today.

This is the town of Napa, founded in 1847, and these days it is booming with culinary activity—and popularity to match. The permanent farmers' market, Oxbow, houses several of the visionary businesses we feature in the pages that follow and serves as a sort of focal point for the town's food scene, along with its "Restaurant Row" on Main Street. Celebrity chefs have joined the burgeoning restaurant landscape, following the lead of local restaurateurs who believed in the town early on, starting businesses there when it was still a city in transition.

From Italian, American, and French to the seafood devotees and artisans of salumi, modern Napa restaurants and chefs are too diverse, too accomplished, and too numerous to name here. Read on for a bit about each of the people who are reshaping the food and wine scene of a town that the entire region is named for.

Angele

540 Main Street
Napa, CA 94559
(707) 252-8115
www.angelerestaurant.com
Owners/Managing Partners: Claude and Bettina Rouas
Executive Chef: Patrick Kelly

Located on the Napa riverfront in a historic 1890s ship chandlery, Angele serves seasonally driven French country cuisine in an elegant, understated environment. Overseen by Bettina Rouas, who hails from a rich heritage of revered hotel and restaurant operators, the restaurant's refined bistro fare and elegant dining room truly do "evoke the simple romance of the classic French brasserie," just as the team describes.

Long before chef Patrick Kelly graduated from The Culinary Institute of America, he discovered at a young age the beauty of food served in an engaging environment. Kelly grew up on his grandparents' farm in Fremont, Nebraska, and worked in the garden and fields tending to livestock. He later pursued a college education at the University of Wyoming, where he discovered he had a passion for food and wine. Soon after, he was drawn to Chicago, New York City, and, ultimately, to the California wine country in pursuit of his craft, superior products, and exceptional wines.

Chef Kelly's desire to be connected to the land, just as in his childhood, has led him to develop relationships with several growers that do "customized growing" at local farms, all located just a stone's throw from the restaurant. Committed to having his finger on the pulse of seasonality, Kelly also drives several times a week to local farmers' markets to search out the best the season has to offer. Farmers from local orchards come to the restaurant every Saturday with apples, pears, and pomegranates, all of which he incorporates into his dynamic menus.

These seasonal—and wine-friendly—menus at the restaurant are just the way Kelly and his team like to eat and drink: good food, great wines, and universally comforting dishes. Kelly and Rouas created a vibrant restaurant where mentoring and teaching young talent has given them great personal rewards. Simply, Angele is founded on a concept of a superb food and wine experience that is both local and simultaneously deeply rooted in European sensibility—particularly the Burgundian and Rhone-style varietals that marry perfectly with the highly flavored ingredients you'll find in the restaurant's dishes.

Angele's team underpromises and overdelivers with big, bold, and aggressive flavors that enable diners to experience a true joy of cooking—showing that simplicity really can speak for itself.

Roasted Hudson Ranch Guinea Hen, Wrapped in Pancetta, with English Peas & Yukon Gold Potato Galette

(SERVES 4)

For the guinea hen:

1 whole guinea hen
Salt and pepper, for seasoning
1–2 pounds pancetta, thinly sliced
6–8 ounces caul fat, as needed for wrapping guinea hen (provided by most butchers)
2 tablespoons butter, for roasting
2 tablespoons canola oil, for roasting

For the guinea hen jus:

Reserved guinea hen carcass, coarsely chopped
2 heads garlic, skin on and crushed
3 heads shallot, peeled and sliced thick
2 cups dry white wine
4 cups poultry or veal stock
2 tablespoons thyme leaves
1 tablespoon rosemary leaves

For the English pea puree:

2 tablespoons butter
¼ cup sliced shallots
½ pound English peas
½ cup heavy cream
Salt and pepper to taste

For the potato galette:

1 large Yukon Gold potato, peeled and julienned
2 eggs
2 tablespoons diced shallots
2¼ teaspoons chopped rosemary leaves
2¼ teaspoons chopped thyme leaves
Salt and pepper to taste
2 tablespoons butter

Have your local butcher quarter the guinea hen, leaving the skin on, and debone the leg and thigh, leaving it intact. Season the meat with salt and pepper and place the exposed flesh side of the breast to the flesh side of the leg and thigh. You should have 2 pieces (each piece totaling half of the guinea hen).

Lay a sheet of plastic wrap on the work surface and lay out the pancetta in lines, overlapping each layer. Place a "piece" of guinea hen toward the bottom of the pancetta and roll the pancetta around to cover, then wrap evenly in caul fat. Repeat step with second "piece" of guinea hen.

Preheat oven to 350°F. Add butter and oil to a heavy-bottomed sauté pan and sear all sides of the hen until golden brown, then place in the preheated oven until the internal temperature of the guinea hen is 155–160°F. Remove from oven and place skin-side up on a drip rack (reserve pan for reheating galette) and let rest 5–10 minutes; set aside, keeping warm for final presentation.

To prepare the jus, preheat oven to 475°F. In a heavy-bottomed saucepot, roast the bones until golden brown. Remove from oven and drain fat. Add the garlic and shallot to the pan and roast an additional 10–15 minutes. Remove the pan from the oven, place on the stove over medium-high heat, and add the white wine. When the wine comes to a simmer, add the stock. Gently simmer and reduce until sauce consistency is achieved, then remove from the burner, add herbs, and steep for 5–10 minutes. Strain jus and reserve for final presentation.

To make the puree, in a small pot over medium heat, melt the butter and add shallots, cooking lightly until tender. Add the English peas and heavy cream and gently heat over medium until peas are tender. Immediately puree the mixture in a blender, then strain through a fine-mesh strainer. Season with salt and pepper; chill and reserve.

To make the galette, place the julienned potatoes in a mixing bowl. Add the eggs, shallots, and herbs and season with salt and pepper to taste; stir to combine. Line a nonstick square or rectangular pan with butter and gently warm. Place the thoroughly combined potato mixture in the pan and gently press down to evenly distribute it. Roast in a 350-degree oven until golden brown and the potatoes are tender throughout. Remove from the pan and let cool to room temperature. Cut the potato into brick shapes and set aside, keeping warm.

While the hen is resting, place the galette in the same pan the hen came out of, and place in the oven to warm. In a small saucepan, gently heat the pea puree. In another sauté pan, warm some seasonal vegetables of your choosing in a little butter and season.

To plate, place a bit of the puree at the base of the plate. Place the galette and seasonal vegetables on the plate as desired. Slice each half of the guinea hen into 4 slices, for 8 pieces total, and arrange 2 slices per plate. Finish with the jus and serve.

DOMAINE CARNEROS

1240 Duhig Road, Napa, CA 94559-9713
(800) 716-2788 · www.domainecarneros.com
Chief Executive Officer/Founding Winemaker: Eileen Crane

Unequivocally one of the most stunning chateaus in wine country, Domaine Carneros sits atop a hill overlooking the expansive Carneros Valley American Viticultural Area (AVA). Domaine Carneros has a strong partnership with the champagne powerhouse, the French estate Taittinger, and their collaboration over the years has produced many outstanding sparkling wine varietals.

Chief executive officer and founding winemaker Eileen Crane knew from an early age that she was destined for the wine business. She grew up in a family that was enamored with French wine, and they flew to France on a regular basis to bring back wines to sample. At age eight she began tasting, using a cordial glass at Sunday dinners.

After graduating from the University of California at Davis, Crane joined Domaine Chandon and began learning the craft of champenoise—traditional sparkling winemaking. She believes this elegant style of winemaking shows off the vineyard and the fruit, enabling a full appreciation of the wine.

At Domaine Carneros, Crane manages 300 acres of vineyards, all estate-grown and 100 percent organic. When they first transitioned to an all-organic system, she says the fruit yield was down 10 to 15 percent the first couple of years—but you could see the vineyards become healthier, more vibrant. Her "coterie of clones" takes five to seven years to mature vines and an additional three to six years in the bottle to produce a mature and integrated vintage.

Though vintage dating in the United States has no requirements, Domaine Carneros vintage dates all sparkling wines; the maker's standard is a full three years from harvest to release. The vintage dating on sparkling wine tells you it was worth aging, Crane explains—this is the difference between vintage and non-vintage labeling that we see on bottles today.

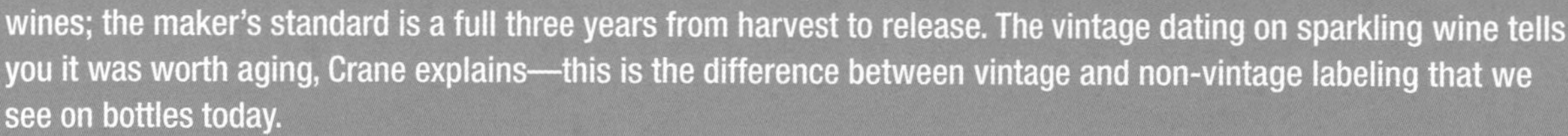

The bubbles in sparkling wine, both large and small, are the result of the injection of carbon dioxide, which acts as a preservative. The CO_2 properly ages the wine for a minimum of three years and as much as six years, giving time for integration between the gas and the wine, creating finer bubbles. Non-vintage is typically only aged eighteen months before release, which, in Crane's opinion, is not enough time for integration—"larger bubbles are more aggressive." With smaller bubbles, you experience a soothing tickle, she says, and a creamy mouth feel.

After working successfully with the Taittinger family for twenty-three years, Crane feels sparkling wine is ideal food wine. "I fell in love for the first time over a bottle of champagne and a filet mignon," she divulges—though she can't promise that same result for everybody.

Auberge du Soleil

180 Rutherford Hill Road
Rutherford, CA 94573
(707) 963-1211
www.aubergedusoleil.com
Executive Chef: Robert Curry

Tucked into the hills that line the picturesque Silverado Trail, in the tiny locale of Rutherford near the town of Napa, the Auberge du Soleil resort and restaurant offers a complete getaway from the daily grind. Whether you stay or dine at this "inn of the sun," you will feel transported, rejuvenated, and renewed—and you will never forget what you had to eat.

Before it was a full-scale resort, the Auberge was conceived of as a dining destination, opened by renowned restaurateur Claude Rouas in 1981 as a Provençal-style establishment in the hills of the Napa Valley. Meant to embody a bit of France and California wine country rolled into one, the Restaurant at Auberge is just that—and it has continued to blossom over the years under the direction of chef Robert Curry. In his seven years at the helm, Curry and his team have repeatedly earned a coveted Michelin star and consistently delight visitors with beautiful dishes that highlight the best of what the region has to offer.

A Los Angeles native, Curry grew up in a close-knit family that treasured food and wine. His father collected wine and his mother was a great cook, so it almost seems inevitable that Curry would grow up to pursue a profession in the culinary arts.

It was at age eighteen while working at Ma Maison, Wolfgang Puck's initial famous LA endeavor, that Curry first took a cooking class—and his eyes opened to the possibilities of the kitchen.

"I was shallow poaching fish and making pastries for the first time," he recalls. This first taste led Curry to enroll at The Culinary Institute of America in Hyde Park, and subsequently to stints at acclaimed restaurants across the United States and throughout France. He says the similarities between France and the Napa Valley are strong.

"The French take a lot of pleasure in eating," he shares, just as food, wine, and hospitality are a huge part of the character of Napa. Seasonality drives his menus, but he's not trying "to get crazy about being organic." Using the best ingredients available, Curry derives inspiration from his extensive travels and especially loves seeing how chefs in other parts of the world interpret simple ingredients at different times of the year. In Paris one winter, for example, "everyone was paying homage to carrots—three chefs and three different three-star restaurants were all doing carrots," he says.

He also loves cookbooks, but is inspired more by the photos than the recipes. "Simplicity goes a long way for me—showing the product for what it is," he explains. No matter what the inspiration, though, Curry says, "It's all about cooking good food for people who enjoy it." And for the self-described fortunate chef who's carrying on a legacy of fine dining, Curry's work at Auberge is something people will continue to enjoy for a long time.

Nantucket Bay Scallops, Quince Stuffing, Brown Butter Vinaigrette

(SERVES 4)

For the butternut squash puree:

2 tablespoons curry powder
¼ cup butter
3 shallots, peeled and minced
3 garlic cloves, peeled and minced
1 small butternut squash, peeled, seeded, and diced
Chicken stock, enough to cover
Salt and pepper to taste

For the verjus-poached quince:

1 quince, peeled, quartered, and cored
2 cups red verjus
1 cup water
¼ cup sugar

For the brown butter vinaigrette (yields 10 ounces):

3 shallots, peeled and minced
¼ pound butter
½ cup hazelnut oil
¼ cup balsamic vinegar
Salt to taste and freshly ground black pepper to taste

For the quince stuffing:

¼ cup cognac
2 tablespoons golden raisins
1 celery stalk, small dice
1½ tablespoons butter
½ garlic clove, peeled and diced
3 thyme sprigs, leaves chopped
1 sage leaf, chopped
12 pieces verjus-poached quince

For the scallops and to plate:

2 tablespoons clarified butter
16 Nantucket Bay scallops
Salt and freshly ground black pepper to taste
1 cippolini onion, blanched, peeled, and quartered
1 tablespoon butter
1 brioche slice, small dice and toasted
1 tablespoon bee pollen for garnish
12 sunflower sprouts for garnish

To make the butternut squash puree, place curry powder in a medium saucepot and toast over low heat. Add butter, shallots, and garlic; sweat until tender. Add squash and chicken stock to cover; season with salt and pepper. Simmer 30 minutes or until squash is tender. Puree in a blender, adjusting consistency with stock.

To make the poached quince, place all the ingredients in a small saucepot. Cover with a clean towel and bring to a simmer. Test for doneness with a paring knife. When the quince gives only the slightest resistance, remove the pot from the heat. Cool to room temperature. Slice the quarters into wedges and the wedges into halves to make 12 pieces total. Reserve the quince in the cooking liquid.

To make the vinaigrette, place the shallots in a large bowl. In a small saucepan, brown the butter and immediately pour over the shallots. Add the remaining ingredients and season to taste.

To make the quince stuffing, boil the cognac in a small pot and pour over the raisins; reserve. Over a low flame, sweat the celery in the butter until translucent. Add the garlic, thyme, and sage and cook for another 3 minutes. Add the 12 pieces of verjus-poached quince and the cognac raisins and heat through.

To prepare the scallops, heat a large sauté pan and add clarified butter. Season scallops on both sides with salt and pepper. Sear scallops, along with the onions, in the hot pan until golden, shaking the pan to flip scallops and onions. Add 1 tablespoon butter to the pan and baste scallops until cooked. Remove from pan onto a paper towel.

To plate, spoon a line of squash puree on each of 4 warm plates. Divide the quince stuffing, onions, and brioche among the plates and place 4 scallops on each plate. Sauce with the brown butter vinaigrette and garnish with bee pollen and sunflower sprouts.

Sautéed Sweetbreads, Philo Gold Apples, Pickled Mustard

(SERVES 4)

For the sweetbreads:

2 leeks
6 stalks celery
12 ounces veal sweetbreads
Salt and freshly ground black pepper to taste
¼ bunch thyme
¼ cup flour
3 tablespoons clarified butter
1 tablespoon butter
3 thyme sprigs
1 garlic clove, skin on, cracked with side of a knife

For the apple butter:

4 Philo Gold apples, peeled, cored, and thinly sliced
6 tablespoons butter
1 teaspoon apple cider vinegar
Salt to taste

For the pickled mustard seeds:

½ cup mustard seeds
1 cup water
¾ cup rice wine vinegar
¼ cup sugar
1½ teaspoons salt

For the mustard seed vinaigrette:

2 tablespoons pickled mustard seeds
1 teaspoon black sesame seeds, toasted
2 teaspoons minced shallots
2 teaspoons chopped chives
½ teaspoon white soy sauce
1 teaspoon lime juice
1 tablespoon extra-virgin olive oil
Freshly ground black pepper to taste

To plate:

1 Pink Pearl apple, peeled, cored, and thinly sliced
2 Flambeau radishes, sliced, for garnish
12 Japanese mizuna leaves for garnish

To make the sweetbreads, preheat oven to 350°F. Chop leeks and celery and place in an ovenproof pan. Season the sweetbreads well with salt and pepper, place on top of leeks and celery, and top with fresh thyme. Cover with aluminum foil and place in the preheated oven for 35–40 minutes. The sweetbreads should be slightly undercooked, as they will be cooked again. When the sweetbreads have cooled sufficiently, remove the connective tissue. Reserve refrigerated.

To make the apple butter, place the apples and butter in a small pot and cover with a lid. Cook over very low heat, stirring occasionally, until the apples are very soft. Blend apples with the apple cider vinegar until they make a smooth, thick sauce. Season to taste with salt.

To make the pickled mustard seeds, place all the ingredients in a small pot. Simmer until mustard "pops" and is no longer crunchy, about 40–50 minutes. Add extra water as necessary to ensure mustard seeds are just covered with liquid.

To make the vinaigrette, combine all vinaigrette ingredients in a small bowl using a whisk.

Heat a large sauté pan. Season the sweetbreads with salt and pepper and dredge in flour. Add clarified butter to the pan and sauté the sweetbreads until golden on one side. Turn the sweetbreads; add 1 tablespoon butter, 3 thyme sprigs, and the garlic clove and baste until golden. Drain on paper towels.

To plate, on each of 4 warm plates, draw a line of apple butter. Divide the sweetbreads among the plates, along each line of apple butter. Place 3 apple slices on each plate. Sauce the plates with the mustard seed vinaigrette and garnish with the sliced radish and mizuna leaves.

Azzurro Pizzeria e Enoteca

1260 Main Street
Napa, CA 94559
(707) 255-5552
www.azzurropizzeria.com
Owners/Proprietors: Michael and Christina Gyetvan
Chef de Cuisine: Steven Hurn

Chef/restaurateurs Michael and Christina Gyetvan moved into this lovely Milan-inspired pizzeria and enoteca—which means "wine library" in Italian—after outgrowing their first restaurant a few blocks away. Sleek and stylish, with lots of natural light, they were eager to continue with their original concept: a restaurant where families, locals, and wine travelers would feel at home.

After training at The Culinary Institute of America in Hyde Park, Michael went on to become chef de cuisine and partner at St. Helena's Tra Vigne restaurant (page 122), working alongside now celebrity chef Michael Chiarello. During that time, downtown Napa started to transform, and Michael had his eye on a space to create his enoteca. What ultimately became Azzurro was built around the stylish brick and tile oven, he says—and it's a great choice. The bright blue-and-white-tile structure commands your attention when you walk in and provides a hearth for this true "locals" restaurant, offering primarily southern Italian cuisine and excellent antipasti dishes.

Michael enjoys the collaboration with chef de cuisine Steven Hurn, whose own résumé is impressive—with time at San Francisco's Delfina and Incanto, among other highly regarded restaurants. Hurn's food style is complementary to the Gyetvans', which focuses on authentic Italian preparations and seasonality with each dish. The team also prepares local favorites like brussels sprouts and caramelized red onions, roasted cauliflower, and grilled shrimp with white beans.

"Still small and to the point" at their new location with its larger kitchen, Azzurro offers fresh and vibrant salads, including a delicious Caesar, along with seasonal baccala (Venetian-style salt cod), homemade meatballs, house favorites (including the shrimp with white beans, sausage, and arugula, featured), and special pastas like the local favorite, baked rigatoni. "We call it the 'lazy man's lasagna' and never consider taking it off the menu," Michael says. "There would be anarchy."

They offer a wide array of specialty Italian cheeses, including Taleggio, Gorgonzola Dolce, pecorino, pepato, burrata, and fresh ricotta, accompanied by a selection of Napa Valley wines and local beer. The team aims to take their show on the road in the summer with a mobile pizza oven and trailer at the Napa farmers' market. "We can enjoy music, beer, and wine—it's sort of a block party featuring local artisans," Michael describes. "I can't think of a better way to spend the day in the wine country."

Grilled Shrimp, White Beans, Sausage & Arugula

(SERVES 4)

1 cup dried white beans
Salt and pepper
6 ounces Italian bulk sausage, thumbnail-size pieces
Extra-virgin olive oil
1 yellow onion, diced fine
1 carrot, diced fine
2 small celery stalks, diced fine
1 tablespoon finely chopped garlic
1 tablespoon butter
1 cup arugula
1 pound 21/25 count Gulf white shrimp, shelled and deveined

Soak the beans in 4 cups water overnight at room temperature. Drain beans. In a large pot, add beans and enough cold water to cover by 1 inch. Add salt and black pepper. Bring beans to a simmer, cover, and cook until tender, about 1 hour. Allow to cool in liquid, then reserve ½ cup liquid and strain beans.

In a sauté pan, cook sausage in 1 tablespoon olive oil until crisp. Add onions, carrots, celery, and garlic and cook until tender. Add beans and the ½ cup cooking liquid and heat until slightly reduced. Add butter and take off heat. When butter is melted, add arugula.

Season shrimp with salt and pepper. Drizzle with olive oil and grill on high heat about 2 minutes per side.

Place bean and sausage mixture in a bowl and top with grilled shrimp.

Bistro Don Giovanni

4110 Howard Lane (formerly Highway 29)
Napa, CA 94558
(707) 224-3300
www.bistrodongiovanni.com
Proprietors: Donna and Giovanni Scala
Executive Chef: Scott Warner

The collaboration of renowned restaurateurs Giovanni and Donna Scala—who opened the original Piatti Ristorante in Yountville and Scala's Bistro in San Francisco—Bistro Don Giovanni bears the owners' names and only gets better every year. This is in part due to the talents of chef Scott Warner, who joined the long-standing Italian bistro in 2002.

Warner will be the first to tell you that food has played a huge part in his life. Heavily influenced by his mother's cooking, he also beams at the mention of culinary icons Julia Child and Jacques Pépin. This early interest in food led to an impressive career, spanning time at restaurants in New York and San Francisco and garnering him and his team a James Beard award for "Best New Restaurant" in the United States at San Francisco's Rose Pistola.

Warner continues to impress with authentic northern and southern Italian dishes at Bistro Don Giovanni. He uses products from the restaurant's on-site gardens and also produces his own grappa and cheese—all part of his work to create rustic peasant foods with a strong connection to their Italian origins and to California's wine country.

The restaurant itself boasts one of the most beautiful dining terraces in the Napa Valley, surrounded by picturesque vineyards and avant-garde sculptures from renowned local artists. The interior is filled with freshly cut flowers and hanging prosciuttos dangling overhead, a reminder of the simply prepared and finely executed dishes coming out of the kitchen.

The wine list is extensive but sensible, well balanced,

and primarily Italian, though with a strong presence of varietals from Napa and Sonoma Counties, including estate-grown wines from the Scalas' personal vineyard. Wine pairing has become a more integral part of the dining experience at the bistro over the years, with menus increasingly crafted around season and climate. For instance, in the summertime, lambruscos and rosés are served with generally simpler food.

Though he travels to truffle festivals in Alba, Italy, it's his farmers in the Napa Valley that inspire Warner today—and he has developed strong relationships with them over his many years as a chef in the Bay Area. He believes in minimizing complexities in his cuisine using "pure ingredients" that are simply prepared. He butchers whole animals for roasting in his brick oven, which he says is his true passion, and treasures the culture honored through his cooking. He loves Ligurian and Tuscan dishes from northern Italy, but says dishes from southern Italy have "a completely different feeling," noting how the seafood, pasta, and tomatoes of Sicily capture a specific cultural experience that has evolved over the centuries.

Warner feels fortunate to be doing what he does each day, and recalls his mother's advice: "Do what you love to do and follow your dreams, wherever they might take you." It's clear that this chef has done just that, with great success—bringing joy to countless diners over the years.

Chicken Parmigiano with Tomato & Zucchini Spaghetti

(SERVES 2)

For the chicken:

1 whole chicken or 2 large, skin-on chicken breasts
4 garlic cloves, thinly sliced
Parmesan bread crumbs
2 eggs
½ cup clarified butter
Salt and pepper to taste

For the Parmesan bread crumbs:

2 cups bread crumbs
1 cup grated Parmesan
Pinch of salt and pepper
¼ teaspoon paprika
1 teaspoon dried oregano

For the zucchini spaghetti:

2 large or 4 small zucchinis
4 large or 8 small ripe red tomatoes
Extra-virgin olive oil, as needed
3 garlic cloves, peeled and smashed with the side of a knife
Salt and pepper to taste
A few torn basil leaves
Handful of basil and parsley leaves
Grated Parmesan for garnish

Preheat oven to 450°F. Debone the whole chicken to two halves, leaving just the first wing bone attached to the breast. Sprinkle the garlic slivers on the meat side of the chicken, not on the skin.

Mix the Parmesan bread crumb ingredients together and place in a shallow pan. Beat the eggs and place in another shallow pan.

Warm the clarified butter in a large sauté pan. Place the chickens skin-side down in the egg wash, then transfer to the bread crumb pan, pushing down on the chicken to fully coat the skin with the bread crumb mix.

Carefully place the chicken skin-side down in the pan without shaking the pan (or the bread crumb mix will fall off when it is baked). Season the chicken with salt and pepper and place in the oven.

While the chicken is cooking, cut the zucchini into long spaghetti-like strands. (Tip: Use a mandoline fitted with the second-to-smallest julienne blade.)

Bring a pot of salted water to a boil. Place the tomatoes in the boiling water for about 1 minute, then carefully remove with a slotted spoon. When cool enough to handle, peel, core, and puree the tomatoes.

In a medium sauté pan, put a few tablespoons of olive oil and the smashed garlic cloves. Over medium heat, toast the garlic slightly, then add the tomato puree. Season with salt, pepper, and a few torn basil leaves. Simmer sauce until slightly thickened. Set aside to keep warm.

When the chicken is almost done (about 30 minutes), place the zucchini in boiling water for about 30 seconds, then remove and place in a strainer to drain.

In a sauté pan, heat a drizzle of good olive oil with the parsley and basil leaves. Add the zucchini to the pan and toss to coat with the oil. Season with salt and pepper, as needed.

To plate, place a thin coat of tomato sauce on each plate, then a small pile of zucchini. Remove the chicken from the oven. Carefully pick up the chicken from the wing-bone side, let the fat drain off, and place on top of the zucchini. Garnish with a sprinkle of grated Parmesan.

Pizza BLT alla Napoletana

(SERVES 2, WITH EXTRA DOUGH FOR FUTURE USE)

For the dough:

4 cups Caputo 00 flour (or equal parts bread flour and all-purpose flour)
2 teaspoons salt
1½ cups tepid water (about 80°F)
½ teaspoon dried yeast

For the pizza:

6–8 ounces pizza dough
¼ cup tomato sauce
2 ounces mozzarella di latte or di bufala, cut into ½-inch-thick strips
6 thin slices of bacon
A couple drizzles (about 1½ tablespoons) of extra-virgin olive oil
1 large tomato, thinly sliced
1 tablespoon grated Parmesan or pecorino
A handful of arugula
A few leaves of basil
Sea salt to taste

Place flour in a mixing bowl. In a separate bowl, dissolve salt in water, then add yeast and stir to dissolve. Add water to flour. Mix either by hand or in a mixer with a dough hook on slow speed, until dough comes together and is slightly sticky yet smooth and elastic (about 5 minutes in the mixer or 10 minutes by hand).

Form a ball of dough and place in a lightly floured bowl. Cover with a damp towel or plastic wrap. Leave outside or in a warm place to proof until smooth and relaxed, about 30 minutes.

Cut dough into 4 pieces and knead into balls. Place balls on a lightly floured sheet pan and cover with a damp towel. Let proof in refrigerator for 1 day before using.

Once proofed, take the dough out of the refrigerator 1 hour before you need it. Note that this recipe tops a single pizza; reserve remaining 3 balls of dough in refrigerator for use within a few days—or in the freezer for use beyond that.

On a floured surface, stretch the dough to desired size, being sure to leave 1 inch unflattened around the edge for the crust to rise higher.

To make the pizza, if a stone-hearth bread or pizza oven is not available, preheat the oven as high as it will go and place a pizza stone or several fire bricks (e.g., the yellow ones typically available at Home Depot) on the bottom shelf. You may also quite effectively use a round Weber charcoal grill with a pizza stone placed on the grill and the lid on top.

Spread the sauce on the dough, again leaving a 1-inch border. Distribute the cheese and bacon evenly on the pizza, drizzle with olive oil, and bake until deep golden brown and crisp.

Garnish the pizza with the tomato slices, grated Parmesan or pecorino, arugula, and basil. Sprinkle with sea salt and another drizzle of olive oil.

Celadon

500 Main Street, Suite G
Napa, CA 94559
(707) 254-9690
www.celadonnapa.com
Chef/Owner: Greg Cole

Chef Greg Cole is a true culinarian. Not only a passionate chef, but also a radio host, wine aficionado, and frequent TV guest, he was also the original Napa maverick, one of the first chefs to bring fine dining to the now popular "Restaurant Row" of the Napa River waterfront. His restaurant, Celadon, which opened in 1996 (when Cole was just thirty-four) in a small building, with a small wine list, has become one of the premier dining destinations in town. And with its gardenlike surroundings and serene atmosphere, it gives a lovely sense of eating in a wine country garden, but with a refined style.

Cole's Napa Valley story began in 1983, when after completing his program at The Culinary Institute of America in Hyde Park, he took a job with famed chef Philippe Jeanty at Domaine Chandon. After that and time in other local restaurants, his interest in winemaking spurred him to work at Robert Sinskey vineyards, a small provincial winery, where he stayed for six years, cooking, working in the cellar, and conducting culinary training seminars showcasing his original food and wine pairings.

The area's growing cadre of great young chefs and focus on ingredient quality, and the difference that makes in great cuisine, are what drew Cole to the Napa Valley—and over the years, his understanding of the connection between quality, the land, and the table has grown. For his seasonally inspired, eclectic cuisine, he seeks out local products from Mark Harber at K&J Orchards and apricots from Green Valley, or olive oil from a Jamison Canyon producer and fresh herbs and vegetables from Sausalito's Spring Farm. When it comes to wine, Cole also relies on local producers he knows well—and openly admits that his personal taste plays a large role. He tends toward local pinot noirs and sauvignon blancs.

After building a loyal local following with Celadon, Cole branched out and opened the highly regarded local steak house, Cole's Chop House, in 2000. It was around the same time that he also decided to buy grapes and American oak barrels to make his own personal cuvée. A bit of a renaissance man, when he's not in the kitchen, Cole can be found spending time with his family, or perhaps even fencing, gardening, or playing his guitar. And his culinary style continues to shape the burgeoning dining scene of the city of Napa.

Soy-Braised Pork Belly & Watermelon with Indonesian Sweet Soy

(SERVES 6)

For the pork belly:

4 cups soy sauce
2 oranges
8 garlic cloves
2 tablespoons chopped fresh ginger
12 black peppercorns
2 pounds pork belly
2 tablespoons canola oil

For the watermelon salad:

1 watermelon, rind removed and flesh diced into ¾-inch pieces
1 watermelon daikon, thinly sliced
1 bunch green onions, thinly sliced on the bias
½ cup rice wine vinegar
Pinch of salt and black pepper

½ cup sweet soy sauce, for finishing the dish

Combine all of the pork belly ingredients, except for the pork belly and canola oil, and bring up to a simmer. Reduce heat and add pork belly, then return to a simmer, keeping pork immersed in braising liquid while cooking. Braise the pork belly until fork tender, approximately 2 hours. It is very important that the braising liquid does not boil; try to keep the temperature around 180°F. When the belly is tender, remove the pan from the heat and allow pork to cool in the braising liquid.

Remove the pork belly from the braising liquid and dice into large, bite-size pieces, approximately ¾-inch square. In a large sauté pan, heat the canola oil and sear the pieces of pork belly, browning on all sides but not cooking too long—it is important not to render the fat.

Combine the watermelon salad ingredients and toss together.

To plate, drizzle sweet soy on the base of a plate and top with watermelon salad. Arrange the pieces of seared pork belly around the watermelon salad.

Flash-Fried Calamari with a Spicy Chipotle Chili Glaze & Pickled Ginger

(SERVES 6–8 AS AN APPETIZER)

For the chipotle chili glaze:

1 (7-ounce) can chipotle chilies in adobo sauce
2 cups orange blossom honey
½ cup rice wine vinegar

For the calamari:

Peanut oil for deep-frying
2 pounds fresh squid, cut into rings
Salt and pepper
1½ cups all-purpose flour
½ cup pickled ginger, sliced
¼ cup chopped chives

Combine the chili glaze ingredients in a blender and process until smooth.

Heat the oil to 375°F. Season the calamari rings with salt and pepper. Toss the squid in the flour to coat evenly and shake off excess. Deep-fry until golden brown, about 2 minutes.

Drain the squid and combine in a bowl with 1 cup of chili glaze, sliced pickled ginger, and chives. Arrange on a platter or on plates with reserved glaze for dipping.

ELYSE WINERY

2100 Hoffman Lane, Napa, CA 94558
(707) 944-2900 · www.elysewinery.com
Winemaker/Owner: Ray Coursen

"Wine is like cooking without a flame," says Ray Coursen, winemaker and owner of Elyse Winery in Napa. "Our heat is the yeast." Coursen is a warm spirit with a ready smile and infectious love of wine, and has a great way of talking about it.

"Wine is food to me," he says, explaining that the philosophy of the winery named for his daughter is slow, cool, gentle treatment of the fruit. This focus on the fruit makes sense given Coursen's University of Massachusetts degree in pomology, the science of stone fruit.

"We're crazy about wine and food here," he says, both of his operation and the region in which it sits. Following a philosophy that "you can't make a million cases taste as good as a thousand," Coursen is devoted to small batches and boutique production. His wines really emphasize the fruit, and they are great with food.

"A meal without wine is eating, but a meal with wine is dining," the winemaker says. When pondering the vineyards they source for their grapes, he continues, "We make our wines with passion . . . with love for the ground, love for the soil," and clearly, love for the end product. Elyse produces mostly reds, predominantly zinfandels and cabernet sauvignons, but also bright, unique white blends and chardonnays that are never over-oaked. Simply, they honor the grapes.

Before he founded Elyse, Coursen worked in a steak house and a wine shop, and then took a job in the tasting room at neighboring winery Whitehall Lane when he moved to California in the 1980s. Eventually, he became a winemaker.

When purchasing wine, Coursen advises people to keep it simple: Find a shop with a good selection and good prices, and make friends with a knowledgeable person who works there. Ask for recommendations.

"To taste good wines, you have to kiss some frogs," Coursen remarks in his classic, direct way. Don't be afraid to explore different pairings, and have fun with it. And whether it be an expensive wine or an affordable, everyday selection, remember to include it when you sit down at the table: It will transform eating into dining.

Fish Story

790 Main Street
Napa, CA 94559
(707) 251-5600
www.fishstorynapa.com
Chefs: Bradley Ogden and Clint Davies

Another new addition to Napa's riverfront dining scene, Fish Story, naturally, is all about fish. The restaurant offers a high-quality, sustainable, seasonal experience with ocean-fresh fish and shellfish, all sourced in accordance with the highly regarded Monterey Bay Aquarium Seafood Watch program. The restaurant is situated downtown in a beautiful stone building, featuring a subtle design and deep-sea-inspired accents as well as great views of the Napa River.

Fish Story's chef, Clint Davies, was born and raised in Tauranga, New Zealand, where fresh seafood was bountiful. He credits his first job, washing dishes in a high-volume restaurant at the tender age of thirteen, for his strong work ethic and describes it as an eye-opening experience. After coming of age, he got more seriously involved with cooking and gradually realized that working with great seafood was what he was meant to do.

Davies traveled to France and Scotland before winning a green card lottery to come to the United States, and he came with a dream: to become a great chef. He bunked with friends in San Francisco while working under Daniel Humm at Campton Place and gravitated toward the cooking style of Bradley Ogden at the Michelin-starred One Market, also in the city. This is where Davies says he connected with the importance of product selection and the critical link between quality ingredients and fresh flavors. He brings this experience to bear at Fish Story.

The restaurant's exciting and well-conceived wine list offers many opportunities to discover great pairings with its food. Davies works daily with general manager Jeremiah Peck and well-known local vintners to ensure the varietals they offer are closely aligned with his cuisine.

Davies—who is focused on creating seasonal, vibrant dishes—is committed and inquisitive, and eager to develop relationships with local growers to get the best products to the plate. He spends time picking fruit and vegetables and draws inspiration from changing his cooking style with the seasons. His aim with Fish Story is to use his experience from cooking in different cultures to keep the menu fresh, while always regional.

Grilled Hawaiian Albacore with Summer Vegetable Barigoule & Spinach

(SERVES 4)

For the vegetable barigoule:

2 lemons
¼ cup peeled and diced carrot, scraps reserved
¼ cup diced celery, scraps reserved
¼ cup peeled and diced yellow onions, scraps reserved
¼ cup diced leek, white part only, scraps reserved
¼ cup diced fennel, scraps reserved
¼ cup olive oil
3 garlic cloves, crushed
1 teaspoon chili flakes
1 teaspoon black peppercorns
1 tablespoon fennel seeds
2 pieces star anise
2 cups white wine
1 cup vegetable stock
¼ bunch rosemary
¼ bunch thyme
2 bay leaves
Salt as needed
1 teaspoon chopped chervil
1 teaspoon chopped parsley
1 teaspoon chopped tarragon
1 teaspoon chopped chives

For the spinach:

4 bunches spinach
1 tablespoon olive oil
Salt and pepper to taste

For the albacore:

4 (6-ounce) pieces albacore fillet
Salt and pepper to taste

To make the vegetable barigoule, halve and juice the lemons; set the juice aside and discard rinds. Dice the carrot, celery, onion, leek, and fennel so they are all the same size; save all the vegetable scraps.

Heat the olive oil in a saucepan and add only the vegetable scraps and crushed garlic; cook slowly over low heat until all ingredients are tender. Add the chili flakes, black peppercorns, fennel seeds, and star anise and cook until they are fragrant. Add the white wine, vegetable stock, rosemary, thyme, and bay leaves and cook until the volume reduces by half. Add the lemon juice and simmer this mixture for 7–10 minutes. Strain and discard the vegetable scraps, reserving the liquid.

Bring the liquid to a boil and season with a generous amount of salt. Add the diced vegetables and cook until tender. Just before serving, add the chervil, parsley, tarragon, and chives. Set aside, keeping warm.

To prepare the spinach, pick the stems off the spinach, discard stems, and wash leaves well. Sauté the spinach in olive oil until wilted. Squeeze out any excess water and divide evenly among 4 bowls. Season with salt and pepper and set aside.

Season the albacore with salt and pepper, grill to your desired temperature, then let the fish rest for 1–2 minutes before slicing each piece into 3 pieces. Place albacore on top of the spinach. Finish by spooning the vegetable barigoule around the spinach and the fish as needed. Drizzle with olive oil just before serving.

Pan-Roasted Halibut with Cherry Tomatoes, Bulgur & Pepper

(SERVES 4)

For the halibut:

4 (6-ounce) pieces halibut
3 tablespoons grapeseed oil, or vegetable oil if unavailable
½ teaspoon sea salt

For the vegetable stock (yields 3 cups):

2 quarts (8 cups) water
¾ cup coarsely chopped yellow onion
¾ cup coarsely chopped celery
¾ cup coarsely chopped carrot
1 head garlic, cut in half
2 bay leaves
½ bunch thyme
Salt and pepper to taste

For the roasted peppers:

4 red peppers
4 yellow peppers
Olive oil to taste
Salt and pepper to taste

For the bulgur:

1 cup bulgur wheat
2½ cups vegetable stock (see recipe)
2 tablespoons butter, unsalted butter
Salt and pepper to taste
Juice of 1 lemon
1 pint cherry tomatoes, cut into halves
½ bunch parsley, chopped

For the roasted red pepper jam:

¼ cup olive oil
2 shallots, peeled and diced
1 garlic clove, crushed
4 roasted red peppers, cut into medium dice
¼ cup sherry vinegar
Sugar to taste

For the yellow pepper puree:

3 tablespoons grapeseed oil
2 shallots, peeled and diced
1 garlic clove, crushed
1-inch piece ginger, peeled and diced
4 roasted yellow peppers
½ cup mirin
½ cup white wine
Salt and pepper to taste

Preheat oven to 350°F. Place the halibut in a preheated skillet with the grapeseed oil just before smoke point, leaving room between the pieces of fish. Sear them to golden brown on one side. Place pan in the preheated oven and cook for 3 more minutes (time may vary depending on size of fish). Flip fish over and cook for 2 more minutes before removing from oven. Set aside, keeping warm.

To make the stock, combine all ingredients in a large stockpot over medium-high heat. Bring to a boil, then reduce to a simmer. Simmer slowly for 1 hour. Strain through a medium-mesh strainer; set aside for the bulgur.

To roast the peppers, rub red and yellow peppers with olive oil, salt, and pepper. Roast in the preheated 350°F oven until the skin begins to blister. Remove from oven and cover, then let sit until skin is easily removable. Remove skin and seeds, dice the peppers, and set aside.

To make the bulgur, boil 2 cups vegetable stock. Remove from heat and add bulgur. Cover and let stand until the stock is absorbed. Heat the bulgur in a sauté pan with butter and a touch of vegetable stock. Season with salt, pepper, and lemon juice. Add cherry tomatoes and chopped parsley to bulgur, and finish with salt and pepper to taste, just before serving.

To make the jam, heat olive oil in a saucepan over low heat. Add shallots and garlic and cook over low heat until translucent. Add red pepper, sherry vinegar, and enough sugar to taste a little sweetness. Bring to a boil, then reduce to a slow simmer and cook until shiny and jam-like consistency.

To make the puree, heat grapeseed oil over low heat. Add shallots, garlic, and ginger and cook over low heat until translucent. Add yellow peppers and cook for about 3–4 minutes, then add mirin and white wine. Increase heat to medium and reduce until only a quarter of the original liquid remains. Remove from heat and add salt to taste. Place contents of the pot into a blender and puree until smooth. Pass through a fine-mesh strainer.

To serve, spoon some puree on one side of the plate. Spread the puree to the other side of the plate by swiping with the heel of a spoon. Distribute the pepper jam and bulgur evenly on all 4 plates. Place the fish on top of the bulgur and finish with a drizzle of olive oil and sea salt.

Hog Island Oyster Company (Oxbow Public Market)

The oyster farm:
20215 Highway 1
Marshall, CA 94940
(415) 663-9218

Napa oyster bar:
Oxbow Public Market
610 First Street
Napa, CA 94559
(707) 251-8113
www.hogislandoysters.com
Chef: Ron R. Stainer

Hog Island Oyster Company is named after a small island in California's Tomales Bay that derives its own unusual name from a fiery shipping incident that released pigs from a cargo hold onto the tiny island, near the coastal town of Marshall. The company is the outgrowth of Florida native Terry Sawyer's passion, along with that of his partners, for "farming the water."

Sawyer grew up on a ranch and moved to the West Coast in 1976 to study marine biology at the University of California at Santa Cruz. He met his future business partners, John Finger and Michael Watchorn, at a party, where the group discovered a shared dream: to cultivate oysters in Northern California. Gradually the dream grew and in 1983 became a reality when the partners, with a loan from their parents, purchased five acres in Tomales Bay and opened their oyster company. While Sawyer was an aquarist at the Monterey Bay Aquarium, his interest in oysters persisted and led him to make weekend trips to plant salvaged oyster seed on the property and help haul the harvest to market.

Of meroir—the sea version of terroir—Sawyer describes what they do at Hog Island as having a "net gain, net benefit" to the environment. The company grows a variety of oyster styles, including European flat, Atlantic, Malpeque, Kumamoto, Pacific, and Olympia oysters, as well as Manila clams and Japanese littleneck mussels. Importantly, they not only sell their freshly farmed products to the public, but also develop delicious, classic dishes around them in their restaurants.

Hog Island's menu at its locations in Napa and San Francisco is lively, concise, and seasonal—always with a focus on quality, freshness, and region. Raw bar selections are reliably fantastic and fresh from the water, while familiar dishes like clam chowder get special Hog Island treatment with in-shell Manila clams and a light broth, to which locals are devoted. The restaurant's wine program naturally focuses on selections that pair well with shellfish, such as sauvignon blanc, chardonnay, and rosé mostly produced by local wineries.

Sawyer—who loves to teach, build community, and is intensely involved with daily production at the oyster farm—prides himself on having a strong connection with both his team and the region. Forming alliances with other hatcheries for seed supply continues to motivate their work.

When it comes to having an oyster experience at home, Sawyer's advice to consumers is to buy from sources with strong reputations—and in the winter, choose Sweetwater or Pacific oysters; in the summer, opt for Kumamoto or Atlantic; and in the fall, European flat oysters are at their best.

Hog Island Seafood Stew

(SERVES 4–6)

For the stew base:

¼ cup extra-virgin olive oil
¼ cup roughly chopped garlic
½ yellow onion, small dice
4 Calabrian chilies, roughly chopped
¼ bunch Italian parsley, roughly chopped
1 tablespoon dried oregano
1 cup white wine
8–10 large tomatoes, peeled, seeded, and roughly diced

For the seafood stew:

¼ cup extra-virgin olive oil
2 pounds Manila or other small clams, rinsed
2 pounds Mediterranean mussels, rinsed and debearded
½ pound wild shrimp, 16/20 count
2 pounds fresh squid, cleaned and cut
2 pounds rock cod or similar, cut into 1-inch cubes
½ cup white wine
Fresh water and kosher salt as needed

Heat the oil, then add the garlic, onion, chilies, and parsley. When garlic is golden, add oregano and wine. Reduce the liquid by half, then add tomatoes and cook for about 30 minutes.

To make the stew, heat the olive oil in a nonreactive pot, large enough to contain all the ingredients. Add all of the shellfish and fish and sauté until color of the cod changes and shells start to open. Add wine and reduce to about a half, then add stew base. If the tomatoes do not have a good amount of juice, you may have to add water; it should be saucy, not soupy.

Cover and allow the ingredients to marry and the stew to slightly thicken. Check for salt and adjust. This dish can be served with your favorite pasta or a grilled piece of crusty bread.

Steamers with Spanish Chorizo

(SERVES 4–6)

For the compound butter:

½ pound butter, softened to room temperature
1 lemon, juice and zest
½ cup thinly sliced garlic, toasted in extra-virgin olive oil
3 Calabrian chilies, finely chopped
1 tablespoon finely chopped dried rosemary
1 tablespoon finely diced shallot

For the steamers:

¼ cup extra-virgin olive oil
1 pound braising greens (chard, kale, escarole, radicchio, etc.)
3 pounds Manila clams or similar, rinsed
1 pound Spanish chorizo (the dry type), cut into ¼-inch pieces
1 cup white wine
1 cup fresh water
Compound butter

Combine all the compound butter ingredients, mix thoroughly, and chill. This should be done ahead of time. The butter can last up to a week in the refrigerator.

Heat the olive oil in a nonreactive pot, large enough to contain all the ingredients. Add the greens, clams, and chorizo and sauté until the greens wilt. Add the wine, water, and butter and cover. It is done once the clams are open. This dish should have a good amount of broth; if it seems dry, you can add more water. You should not have to add salt due to the saltiness of the clams and the chorizo.

Hog Island Manila Clam Chowder

(SERVES 6)

1 tablespoon butter
3 fresh thyme sprigs
1 pound high-quality bacon, sliced
1 large carrot, peeled and thinly sliced
1 small stalk celery, thinly sliced
1 large leek, white part only, thinly sliced on the diagonal
3 medium Yukon Gold potatoes, peeled and cut into bite-size cubes
2 pounds small, raw Manila clams in the shell, rinsed
3 cups heavy cream
Salt and pepper
Parsley for garnish

In a large, heavy-bottomed pan, melt the butter with the thyme. Add the bacon and render it completely, without burning it. Add the carrots and cook until they are semisoft, then add the celery and leeks and cook until the celery has lost its crunch.

In another pot, bring about 5–6 cups of water to a boil and cook the potatoes until they are soft. Then add the potatoes and about 4 cups of the potato cooking water to the bacon and vegetables and bring to a boil.

Place some of the clams in a sauté pan over medium heat. (You will need to do this in batches.) Ladle about 1 cup of the chowder base on top and cover the pan. Cook for 5 to 7 minutes or until most of the clams are open, pick through and discard any unopened ones. (Don't skip this step—the unopened clams were dead going into the pot and could spoil the chowder.)

Add the cooked clams back to the chowder base, and repeat until all the clams are cooked. Add ½ cup cream per serving and bring the chowder to a boil. If it is too thick, add more of the potato water.

When the chowder is bubbling in the middle, it is ready. Adjust the seasoning with salt and finish the soup with cracked pepper and chopped parsley.

FATTED CALF
(OXBOW PUBLIC MARKET)

644 C First Street, Napa, CA 94559
(707) 256-3684 · www.fattedcalf.com
Chefs/Owners: Toponia Miller and Taylor Boetticher

An artisanal charcuterie and butcher shop that opened in 2008, the Fatted Calf is the realization of the dream of chefs/owners Toponia Miller and Taylor Boetticher, a married couple whose shared goal was to master the art of crafted meat. Miller is a Culinary Institute of America grad who was most inspired by her charcuterie class; Boetticher had cured meats at Berkeley's Cafe Rouge and sold salumi at the local farmers' market. The idea to open a shop was born in San Francisco's Dogpatch neighborhood, located in the city's meatpacking district, where they shared a small space with a little walk-in and aging room for their curing of regional farmstead meats.

After marrying, the couple traveled to Italy, where they lived for a time, deepening their knowledge of the art of European-style cured meats—and working for famous Chianti butcher Dario Cecchini, honored in Bill Buford's excellent book on the world of professional cooking, *Heat*. This intimate experience in another culture gave the couple an understanding of family-driven ancestral traditions that is evident in their products today.

The couple's philosophy is simple: Use old-world methods, handcrafting each individual product in small batches with the highest quality ingredients (their meats are all organic and hormone-free). These beautiful sausages, pâtés, salumi, prosciutti, and confits have become hugely popular via all of the Fatted Calf stores—after their first brick-and-mortar in Napa's Oxbow Public Market, where they do most of their curing and processing, they subsequently opened two other retail shops in nearby San Francisco.

Miller and Boetticher constantly expand their repertoire, producing pickles and sauerkraut and doing whole animal butchery. Current daily production includes six pâtés, twelve salami, and seven or eight muscle cuts from duck, quail, goose, and pork. In the summer, they prepare Basque grilling sausage and quail stuffed with figs and sausage, and in the winter, products like chestnut-studded boudin blanc (a white sausage traditionally made with chicken and pork) make their way onto shop shelves.

The couple is grateful to be a part of the wine country food community, and recently built a wood-burning oven together at their home to continue exploring artisanal traditions in their downtime.

La Toque

1314 McKinstry Street
Napa, CA 94559
(707) 257-5157
www.latoque.com
Chef/Owner: Ken Frank

With its wood-burning fireplace, warm earth tones, and stylish decor, La Toque is the pinnacle of wine country sophistication. The restaurant, which is adjacent to the beautiful Westin Verasa Napa hotel, is elegant, comfortable, and the perfect venue to experience chef and owner Ken Frank's Michelin-starred cuisine.

One of the region's most influential and celebrated chefs, Frank, as a child, loved to cook with his grandfather—who was a butcher by day and an inventor by night—and make candy together that they would share with neighbors. He attended school in Geneva while working at a local hotel, filleting fish and washing dishes. Upon return to the United States, he continued work in the kitchen, cooking with several great European chefs in Los Angeles, where he soon realized what his future was meant to be.

As chef de cuisine at La Guillotine, Frank got noticed—a young American chef preparing superb French food was not the norm in the area at the time. And when he was just twenty-four, in 1979, he opened the original La Toque, to great acclaim. The restaurant was soon recognized by the New York Times and Los Angeles Times, and diners had to make reservations a month in advance.

Yearning for a more food- and wine-focused area, after traveling the world, Frank selected the Napa Valley—a place he feels is "paradise." The fit was a perfect one for his desire to cook with the best seasonal ingredients and see the farmers, cheesemakers, and food artisans each day.

He crafts his menus by season and has learned to anticipate what's available. An avid duck hunter, he holds special dinners for other duck hunters at the restaurant in the winter. And he has always been fascinated by wine, which he says starts with the ultimate great ingredient, the wine grape. His wine-friendly style of cooking forgoes spicy combinations to focus on harmonious flavors, as opposed to contrasting ingredients.

La Toque boasts more than 2,000 wines on its international list—including many food-friendly pinot noirs—with a team of three sommeliers to advise diners on the most complementary picks with their meals. As a mentor to many young chefs in the area, Frank shares his philosophy: Trust Mother Nature, be true to yourself, and use sensible combinations—always try to refine techniques, but don't try to be different just to be different. This commitment to authenticity has certainly been the right choice for him, and for the huge following of loyal diners he has acquired over the years.

New England Skate Wing Sautéed with Parsnip Puree, Almonds & Brown Butter

(SERVES 4)

Skate wing is delicate, delicious, and easy to cook but it is extremely perishable, especially once it has been filleted. Buy it the day you plan to cook it from a good fishmonger who can properly cut it for you.

For the skate wing:

4 (6- to 8-ounce) pieces fresh skate wing, filleted and skinned
Salt for seasoning skate
Flour for dredging
¼ cup canola oil, to cook skate
¼ cup unsalted butter, plus 1 little nib to test the oil
⅓ cup peeled and sliced almonds
Juice of 1 lemon

For the parsnips:

1½ cups peeled and sliced parsnip
2 tablespoons unsalted butter
Salt to taste

Season the pieces of fish with salt on both sides. Dredge in the flour and pat off excess. Heat the canola oil in a large sauté pan with a small nib of butter. As soon as the butter begins to brown, the oil is the right temperature to add the fish. Cook the fish over fairly high heat, about 90 seconds on each side; it should be light golden brown. When done, remove the fish from the pan and place on paper towels to absorb any excess oil.

Drain the oil from the pan, wipe it out well, and return the still very hot pan to the heat. Add the remaining ¼ cup butter to the pan; it should sizzle and brown fairly quickly. As soon as it browns, add the sliced almonds and cook another 30 seconds, then add the lemon juice and remove from heat.

Gently sauté the sliced parsnips in a small pan with 2 tablespoons butter, stirring frequently until they begin to turn golden brown. Season with a good pinch of salt, add a splash of water, cover tightly, and let parsnips cook over very low heat, just simmering, for another 10 minutes. They should be very tender. Puree in a food processor, verify seasoning, and keep warm.

To serve, place each piece of skate in the center of a plate on a spoonful of the parsnip puree. Spoon brown butter and almonds over the top. Bon appétit!

Rutherford Ribs Braised in Red Wine, Fiscalini Pearl Tapioca & Baby Carrots

(SERVES 4)

For the short ribs:

1 tablespoon butter
1 cup mirepoix (2 parts onion, 1 part carrot, and 1 part celery—all peeled and diced)
2 tablespoons tomato paste
2 tablespoons flour
1 (750-ml) bottle cabernet sauvignon
4 (8-ounce) pieces beef short ribs, boneless
Salt and pepper to taste
Cooking oil as needed
2 cups veal stock

For the carrots and cauliflower:

12 baby carrots, peeled
½ cup cauliflower florets
2 cups water
2 tablespoons butter
1 teaspoon sugar
½ teaspoon sea salt

For the tapioca:

½ cup finely diced white onion
1 tablespoon canola oil
¾ cup large-pearl tapioca
2 teaspoons salt
⅓ cup dry white wine
⅔ cup water
1 cup milk
¾ cup heavy cream
1½ cups grated white cheddar cheese (Fiscalini preferred), packed tightly

Put the butter and mirepoix in a large saucepan and cook over moderate heat for 3–4 minutes, stirring from time to time until the vegetables just begin to turn golden brown. Add the tomato paste and flour, stir well, and then deglaze with cabernet sauvignon.

In the meantime, season the short ribs with salt and pepper. Heat a separate sauté pan with a little cooking oil and sear the ribs on all sides until rich golden brown.

Add the seared ribs to the pan with the wine and vegetables, add the stock, cover, and bring to a boil. Once at a boil, reduce the heat to maintain a gentle simmer for at least 2 hours, until the ribs are "fall off the bone" tender.

Carefully remove the meat from the braising liquid and keep warm. Strain the sauce, allow to settle for a few minutes, and skim off any fat. Reduce to a nice, rich consistency. Verify and adjust seasoning if necessary before serving.

Over medium heat, cook the carrots and cauliflower in gently boiling water, with butter, sugar, and a pinch of salt until tender and lightly glazed (approximately 3 to 5 minutes).

To make the tapioca, lightly cook the onions in canola oil on low heat until tender but not colored. Add tapioca and salt and stir together as if making rice pilaf. Add white wine and water and bring to a simmer over moderate heat, stirring frequently to prevent sticking. When half of the liquid is absorbed, add milk and cream and bring back to a simmer. Remove from heat, cover, and let sit for 30 minutes to allow the tapioca to soften.

Return the tapioca to moderate heat, add the grated cheese, and cook at the lowest simmer possible, stirring constantly for 5 minutes. Remove from heat and cover for another 20 minutes until the pearls are translucent. Verify seasoning and adjust consistency with a little milk if the tapioca is too thick.

To each of four individual plates, add an ample portion of tapioca, place short ribs on top of tapioca, and spoon reduced sauce over the top, covering it completely. Add glazed carrots and cauliflower and serve.

Norman Rose Tavern

1401 First Street
Napa, CA 94559
(707) 258-1516
www.normanrosenapa.com
Chefs/Owners: Michael and Christina Gyetvan
Chef de Cuisine: Douglas Seeley

Norman Rose Tavern is located in the heart of downtown Napa, an area presently undergoing a major resurgence in popularity due to burgeoning development in town. The second successful venture of Michael and Christina Gyetvan (the first, Azzurro Pizzeria e Enoteca, page 142), Norman Rose is the product of Michael's desire to build a tavern and produce dishes he says he wants to eat when he's cooking.

"I believed in downtown Napa as a destination," Gyetvan shares, "and I wanted to open a neighborhood place that had an old tavern feel."

He's successfully achieved that with Norman Rose, which features tavern-style classics with locally sourced products. With chef Douglas Seeley at the head of the kitchen, Norman Rose offers well-executed comfort foods like lamb burger with herbed goat cheese or Caggiano bratwurst with house-made sauerkraut.

"We are fortunate to have such easy access to products," Gyetvan says. They "love and respect" local farms, including Hudson Ranch for pigs, Five Dot Ranch for beef, and local lamb sourced from the Sonoma coast since they opened their doors.

Keeping with the local theme, the tavern pours classic beers and strictly domestic wines from Napa and Sonoma. As Gyetvan explains, "We have created an approachable list with a good rotation of vintages and varietals—most are classic wines from our region, such as sauvignon blanc, chardonnay, zinfandel, and cabernet sauvignon and Italian varietals grown domestically, such as primitivo, ribolla gialla, and refosco." These varietals marry well with the tavern fare, he says—and we agree.

Gyetvan, a Culinary Institute of America graduate, fondly remembers dining at Alice Waters's Chez Panisse long ago, which he says set things off and running. "All I wanted at that stage in my career was to be part of the new American food movement."

During his time at Tra Vigne, he became part of that movement, learning to make extra-virgin olive oil from local olives and curing and aging prosciutto, but he also learned about business. After leaving Tra Vigne and traveling throughout the United States opening concept establishments for a successful restaurant company, he grew tired of travel and yearned to stay put—and opened a small pizzeria in downtown Napa on a credit card budget.

From those humble beginnings developed a family of six, plus a redbone coonhound named Rufus, who all love food—Gyetvan describes them as "free spirits." And the character of these free spirits comes through in their restaurants and in the classic, comforting, and fun food of Norman Rose, named after both sides of the family (and the couple's children bear these middle names). Keeping with the family theme, all of the pictures in the restaurant are family photographs, ones that the Gyetvans and their guests have come to cherish over the years.

Norman Rose Tavern Grilled Lamb Burgers

(SERVES 4)

For the herbed goat cheese:

½ pound fresh chèvre (goat cheese)
1 tablespoon minced chives
1 tablespoon chopped parsley
1½ teaspoons minced tarragon
1½ teaspoons chopped thyme
1 teaspoon roasted garlic paste

For the sautéed spinach:

1 tablespoon olive oil
1 tablespoon finely chopped garlic
1 bunch fresh spinach (or about a 12-ounce bag of washed spinach)
Salt and pepper to taste

For the burgers:

½ red onion, finely diced
3 garlic cloves, finely chopped
3 tablespoons extra-virgin olive oil
½ teaspoon cumin seeds, toasted and ground
¼ teaspoon ground cinnamon
2 tablespoons red wine
2 pounds ground lamb
Salt and freshly ground black pepper to taste
4 hamburger buns

To make the herbed goat cheese, whip the cheese using an electric mixer until it begins to soften. Mix in the herbs and garlic paste. You may need to thin the mixture with a splash of cream or water depending upon the moisture content of the cheese. It should be a creamy, spreadable consistency.

To make the spinach, heat the oil in a large sauté pan, add the garlic, and swirl it around until it begins to turn a toasty golden brown color. Add the spinach and wilt; season with salt and pepper.

To make the burgers, sauté the onion and garlic in the extra-virgin olive oil. Cook for 3–4 minutes until softened. Add the spices and then deglaze with the red wine. Continue cooking until the wine has evaporated. Spread the mixture onto a plate and allow to cool.

Mix the onion mixture into the ground lamb and form 4 8-ounce patties. Season both sides with salt and freshly ground black pepper and grill or griddle to desired doneness.

While the lamb is grilling, toast 4 hamburger buns of your liking. Spread the bottom of the bun liberally with the herbed goat cheese. Top with the cooked lamb patty and then finish with a nice mound of the sautéed garlicky spinach.

OENOTRI

1425 FIRST STREET
NAPA, CA 94559
(707) 252-1022
WWW.OENOTRI.COM
CHEFS/OWNERS: CURTIS DI FEDE AND TYLER RODDE

Meaning "vine cultivators," the word oenotri feels like the right name for this southern Italy–focused restaurant in the heart of old Napa. The menu changes daily, features house-made salumi and pastas, and "celebrates culinary traditions rarely seen elsewhere in California—the specialties of Sicily, Campania, Calabria, Basilicata, and Puglia." And the character of the restaurant seems to embody that of its two young chefs, Curtis Di Fede and Tyler Rodde, the vine cultivators themselves.

The pair first met while working at the acclaimed Oakland restaurant Oliveto under Paul Bertoli, where they also truly discovered a love of Italian cooking—and they have since taken the local food world by storm. Both Napa natives, they returned to their hometown to open Oenotri in 2010 as an outlet for their love of southern Italian cuisine. Di Fede is a graduate of La Cordon Bleu in London and was initially inspired to cook by his Sicilian great uncle (also, his great grandfather managed the famous Beringer winery, page 107). Rodde, a graduate of the California School of Culinary Arts, hails from a family with deep roots in the wine industry and traveled to most European wine-growing regions as a young man.

With this pedigree, it's not surprising that Oenotri gets it right. The restaurant is both approachable and refined, with a modern, hip decor and a staff that is well versed in

articulating the chefs' vision. Whether producing ricotta or mascarpone or butchering a whole pig each week to make its way into fifteen varieties of house-made salumi, it's clear that having access to their own four-plus-acre farm has its benefits. They also produce olive oil from olives hand-harvested from the 200 trees on their nearby farm, and, on most afternoons, you'll find the chefs planting heirloom seeds or tilling and harvesting produce from the farm themselves.

Oenotri offers an exceptional wine list of predominantly Italian varietals, which, by the chefs' own admission, causes debate and discussion given their location in California wine country. With 650 labels presently on the list, diners can find both an old- and new-world selection that marries perfectly with each dish. And every one of those dishes captures the essence of wine country—whether it's Napa or Italy—and of that special connection between the chefs, the land, the ocean, and the farm.

Seared King Salmon with Sweet Corn & Cherry Tomatoes

(SERVES 4)

For the salmon:

4 (6-ounce) portions Pacific king salmon (skin-on is optional)
2 tablespoons olive oil
Pinch of sea salt

For the sweet corn:

4 ears corn
1 pint cherry tomatoes, cut into halves
12 basil leaves (about 2 sprigs)
1 garlic clove, peeled and mortared into a paste
Sea salt to taste
2 tablespoons unsalted butter

Preheat oven to 300°F. Take the salmon and feel around for any bones that your fishmonger might have missed. Portion the salmon as close as you can to 6 ounces apiece.

Heat a large nonstick sauté pan to medium-high. Once the pan is hot, add the olive oil and wait until the oil is almost smoking. Season the salmon with sea salt on the skin side, then place it skin-side down in the pan. Sear the salmon, on the skin side, until it has an opaque color about ¼ inch up the side of the fish. Remove the salmon from the pan and place it skin-side up on a baking sheet. Place the salmon in the oven and bake for about 12 minutes.

Clean and cut all the kernels off the cobs. In the pan that the salmon was in, add the corn kernels and sauté for about 8 minutes. Remove from the heat and add the cherry tomatoes, basil leaves, garlic paste, and sea salt. Return pan to heat and add butter to the corn and tomatoes. Cook until butter is well incorporated and melted.

Remove the salmon from the oven and plate as desired with the corn and tomato garnish.

Oxtail Braise with Pappardelle Pasta

(SERVES 4)

For the fresh pappardelle pasta:

2 whole large eggs
2 egg yolks
2 cups type 00 flour

For the oxtail:

2 cups flour
Salt and pepper
6 pounds oxtail, cut into chunks
¼ cup extra-virgin olive oil
4 garlic cloves, mashed in salt to puree consistency
1 red onion, chopped
1 cup red wine
3 cups crushed tomatoes with juice
Beef stock to cover
2 bay leaves
1 tablespoon cumin
1 tablespoon coriander
1 teaspoon cinnamon

To make the pasta, in a small bowl, crack 2 whole eggs and add the 2 egg yolks.

Place the flour in a separate, large bowl and add the eggs and yolks one at a time, whisking with a fork. Once all is incorporated, wrap up the dough in plastic and let it rest in the refrigerator for 30 minutes.

Remove dough from refrigerator and roll out with a pasta-rolling machine on the thinnest setting. Cut pasta into 8-inch-long and ½-inch-wide noodles.

To prepare the oxtail, place the flour in a shallow bowl and season with salt and pepper. Dredge the meat in the flour, shaking off any excess.

In a large stockpot over high heat, add the olive oil. When the oil is hot, add the meat and brown on all sides, about 3 minutes per side. When all of the meat is browned, remove the meat from the pan and set aside on a plate.

Add to the pot the garlic and onion and cook until translucent, then add the wine. Add the browned meat back into the pot, along with the crushed tomatoes, enough beef stock to cover the meat, and the bay leaves, cumin, coriander, and cinnamon. Bring to a simmer over low heat for 2½ hours. Remove from heat and let cool.

Once cool, pick the oxtail off the bone and return all of the meat to the braising liquid. Reheat the desired portion of oxtail braise in a large sauté pan.

Meanwhile, bring a tall pot of water to a boil for the pasta. Add the pappardelle to the boiling water. Once the pappardelle is al dente (after approximately 5 minutes), add it to the sauté pan with the oxtail. Toss gently and finish with extra-virgin olive oil.

Restaurant Cuvée

1650 Soscol Avenue
Napa, CA 94559
(707) 224-2330
www.cuveenapa.com
Executive Chef: Jordan Mackey

Not far from Napa's bustling Oxbow Public Market, Restaurant Cuvée has both the feeling of a sophisticated farmhouse and the cozy comfort of a living room. The gorgeous space is the perfect venue for the distinctive style of chef Jordan Mackey, which he describes as "high country cuisine."

"I always try to let the property speak to me, and this building really has an urban farmhouse feel," Mackey explains. "It's on a winery, but in a city. It feels a little bit low-country, but not southern. So I wanted to embody the 'country' part of wine country, and build on that with some reinvented country classics—with a 'high cuisine' spin."

Although not the first person to use this concept, it feels like a perfect match for Mackey's talent and the restaurant's agriculturally abundant Northern California location.

Mackey arrived in the area in 2010 with a desire to connect with the land and "put his hands on" where food comes from. He says it's been both a challenge and a privilege to participate in a culture centered around great farms and wineries—it wasn't long before farmers were showing up at the restaurant's back door with stone fruits, figs, plums, mandarins, and goat cheese. He was even able to meet the goats of Sky Hill Farm, which produce this incredible cheese.

The chef executes this concept flawlessly, with dishes that feel good for the soul and that highlight emotionally resonant flavors. Mackey designs dishes for a sensory experience and strives for flavors that take you back to your roots—for instance, parsnips and honey with short ribs, a comforting, luscious, elevated combination. He cooks with local wineries in mind, using products like single varietal, unfermented sauvignon blanc juice for a vinaigrette or pastry preparations involving black muscat on figs and house-churned ice cream.

Wine is an inherent part of the Cuvée experience. A recipient of Wine Spectator's Award of Excellence, the impressive wine list reflects relationships with both established and newer producers, all based in the Napa Valley. They even offer both a wine-on-tap and barrel tasting program, giving the diner the rare opportunity to taste special blends or varieties not often available at other venues.

With the wine ever important, Mackey also has plans to deepen the restaurant's food-land connection: He started an organic garden and will soon have a full composting program for a "full-cycle" food experience. His commitment to connecting with the land is serious—Mackey even spent one winter tracking the sun to determine the best arrangement of his chef's garden for the following year. He is clearly achieving his goal of connecting with the food source, and his stylistic country-inspired dishes, which showcase the best wine country ingredients, demonstrate a concept that is a true testament to the beauty of simplicity and quality combined.

Spice-Roasted Beef Strip Loin with Potatoes 3 Ways, Chanterelles, Spicy Tomato Jam & Natural Jus

(SERVES 6)

For the beef strip loin:

6 (14-ounce) portions beef strip loin
¼ piece of cinnamon stick
3 cloves
4 white peppercorns
2 allspice berries
Kosher salt
Olive oil, as needed

For the vegetables, mushrooms, and beef sauce:

15 marble-size rainbow potatoes, halved
1 bulb fennel, sliced into strips, trim reserved
¼ cup olive oil
Sea salt
24 small chanterelle mushrooms
½ pound Bloomsdale spinach
1 quart (4 cups) rich beef stock

For the potato sauce:

¼ cup butter
1 russet potato, diced into small cubes
Fennel trim
1 small shallot, chopped
1 small leek, chopped
2 cups water
1 cup heavy cream
Salt

For the tomato jam:

4 large very ripe tomatoes, peeled, seeded, and chopped
1 teaspoon chopped ginger
3 tablespoons rice vinegar
1 teaspoon chili flakes
1 teaspoon kosher salt
2 tablespoons sugar

For the fried potatoes:

2 cups vegetable oil, for frying
1 marble-size rainbow potato, thinly sliced

Clean all fat and gristle from the strip loin. Roast the spices and grind in a spice grinder. Very lightly dust beef portions with ground spices and some kosher salt. Pan-roast in a sauté pan in a little olive oil until well seared on both sides. Finish in the oven to desired temperature.

To make the vegetables, mushrooms, and beef sauce, toss the potato halves and fennel in 2 tablespoons olive oil and sea salt. Roast on a cookie sheet until tender and well roasted, then add chanterelles and roast for 7 minutes more. Sauté spinach in 2 tablespoons olive oil and season with salt (be careful not to overcook spinach, as it will release a lot of water). Reduce beef stock to a thick and syrupy consistency; reserve.

To make the potato sauce, melt 2 tablespoons butter and add cubed potatoes, fennel trim, shallot, and leek. Sweat vegetables until very tender and fragrant. Add water, cover, and steam until potatoes are tender. Add heavy cream and bring to a boil. Remove from heat and transfer to

a blender. Blend at medium speed and add 2 tablespoons butter. Season with salt and reserve.

To make the jam, combine all the ingredients in a medium saucepan over medium heat. Reduce, stirring often, until very dry and thick. Transfer to a blender and puree at high speed until smooth. Reserve.

To serve, place a bed of spinach in the center of a plate and arrange sliced beef over the spinach. Swirl a ribbon of potato sauce around the plate. Evenly distribute the potatoes and chanterelles around the beef. Drizzle some beef stock reduction on top of the potato sauce and over the beef. Take the sliced potatoes and deep-fry at 320°F in 2 cups olive oil until golden and crisp, and top finished dish.

VINTNER'S COLLECTIVE

1245 Main Street, Napa, CA 94559
(707) 255-7150 · www.vintnerscollective.com
Owners: Garret and Kim Murphy

The historic stone building that once housed a brewery, a saloon, a Chinese laundry, a butcher shop, a feed store, and a brothel—the Pfeiffer building, built in 1875—is now home to Vintner's Collective, a wonderful multi-winery tasting room in downtown Napa.

Proprietor Garret Murphy, who was born in Boston in 1967 but grew up in Paris, was influenced early on by his parents, who were passionate about wine. His Harvard grad father had a driving passion to live the "joie de vivre" and shared that passion with all of his sons. The family bottled vats of wine at home and discussed wine-growing regions like Alsace, Bordeaux, and Burgundy. Following this enlightened childhood, Murphy started professional work in food as a pastry chef, but says his transition to wine was seamless.

He met his future wife, Kim, who has family in Napa, while she was studying at the Parsons School of Design in Paris. Before the Murphys opened Vintner's Collective, Garret spent time at a variety of distinguished establishments, including as pastry chef and consultant at Meadowood Napa Valley and with Jean-Noel Fourmeaux of Chateau Potelle on Mount Veeder, in the tasting room. He began to focus more on winery operations, and networking with local vintners enabled him to open a Napa tasting room. Murphy envisioned sharing the space with other vintners and small boutique wineries and joining them together in a true collective, partnering to launch their wineries and build a following with the public.

"We want our customers to find extraordinary and unique wines in the tasting room," Murphy says. Tasting and pairings happen daily to experience up to eighteen different wines available at any given time in the collective; members receive wine up to five times a year.

Vintner's Collective provides a unique opportunity to experience some up-and-coming special Napa Valley appellations. Over the last decade there has been an ongoing search for new places in the region to find unique appellations. One example is Coombsville, an area bearing fruit that is being strongly considered the next superior AVA due to the character of the terroir and the area's diverse microclimates.

When considering a bottle of wine to drink, Murphy advises checking for cork taint—a moldy, musty, or earthy flavor that dominates the fruit and aroma of the wine, reducing its overall appeal. It can make a wine that is usually vibrant with fruit-forward characteristics "frozen in time" or flat—in other words, the wine has been stressed in the bottle and no longer "talks" to you. Wine, Murphy explains, should show character that is full with well-balanced tannins. So, trust your judgment—and for the latest in exciting new Napa Valley wines, head to Vintner's Collective for a tasting.

SIENA

875 Bordeaux Way
Napa, CA 94558
(707) 251-1900
www.themeritageresort.com/siena-restaurant.php
Chef: Michael Collins

Located in the magnificent Meritage Resort, which sits at the mouth of the Napa Valley, Siena is an inviting place. The restaurant echoes the design of the resort, which captures the style of old-world Tuscany. The entire property offers a truly magical environment, complete with a spectacular winery, a tasting room out the back door of the beautifully appointed restaurant, and a luxurious spa that is built into the hillside vineyard.

Siena's chef, Michael Collins, grew up in an Italian family and spent most days as a child in the kitchen with his mother and grandmother, cooking what he describes as "old school" sauces, pastas, and desserts. Collins began cooking professionally at a young age, in Lake Powell, Utah, where he was soon offered an apprenticeship at the famed Greenbrier Resort. He went on to the Ritz Carlton, St. Regis, and the Bacarra resort in Santa Barbara, and recently joined the team at the Meritage with a clear vision to elevate the cuisine to new heights.

In Collins's Californian-Italian-style cuisine at Siena—where he says he has a lot of freedom to tell his story—ingredients play a huge part in how he accomplishes a blend of simplicity and well-defined flavor profiles. He visits farmers' markets regularly while developing and cultivating his new one-acre chef's garden, slated to provide excellent ingredients for menus directly from the field, where diners will "taste the quality on the plate."

The chef enjoys the wine experience, too—he showcases the wine on his list by offering white, red, and dessert wine flights. He actually beams with pride when talking about his collaboration with director of winery operations Garrett Busch and winemaker Kevin Mills, and is incredibly proud of their on-site winery, Trinitas Cellars. It is a working vineyard, designing an approachable wine that's well balanced and drinkable, and expected to be "fun and educational."

In addition to further developing Siena's menus, Collins is working with his operations team to expand the property with an additional 250 rooms as well as two new dinner-only restaurants, designed to be hip and fun, with simple food and ingredients that people will understand. Crush, the property's new gastro-pub, is now open, as is an upscale bakery and Italian-style coffee shop, Blend Cafe. With all this growth, it feels like a great time for a wine country visit.

Black Trumpet Mushroom-Crusted Beef Tenderloin, Potato Puree & Glazed Carrots

(SERVES 4)

For the beef tenderloin:

4 (6-ounce) beef tenderloin steaks
Salt and black pepper to taste
¼ cup all-purpose flour
4 eggs, beaten
½ cup black trumpet or chanterelle mushrooms, dried and ground
2 ounces olive oil

For the glazed carrots:

8 peeled baby carrots
2 cups water
1 teaspoon sugar
½ teaspoon salt
1 tablespoon butter

For the potato puree:

1 pound Yukon Gold potatoes, peeled and cut in quarters
½ cup cream
3 tablespoons butter

Preheat oven to 350°F.

Season steaks with salt and pepper. Lightly dust one side with flour, then coat floured side with beaten eggs and crust with mushrooms. Heat oil in a large sauté pan on high heat and sear mushroom crust. Transfer steaks to the preheated oven and bake until medium-rare, about 8 minutes. Let rest 5–8 minutes before serving.

Cook carrots in a medium saucepan with water, sugar, salt, and butter. Cook until tender and remove from heat; set aside, keeping warm.

Place potatoes in salted, boiling water and cook over medium heat until tender. Strain through a colander and let drain for 3 minutes. Place back into pot with cream and butter, mixing thoroughly until smooth. Set aside, keeping warm.

On a serving plate, place an ample portion of potato puree. Place tenderloin and carrots on plate as desired and serve.

Mustard-Glazed Ahi Tuna with Dungeness Crab, Fava Bean & Roasted Cauliflower Salad & Green Olive Pesto

(SERVES 4)

For the tuna:

1 teaspoon mustard seeds
1 teaspoon stone-ground mustard
4 (4-ounce) portions ahi tuna
1 tablespoon olive oil

For the crab, fava bean, and cauliflower salad:

½ pound cauliflower
3 tablespoons olive oil
Salt and pepper
¼ cup mayonnaise
¼ cup crème fraîche
2 tablespoons minced chives
2 tablespoons fresh lemon juice
1 ounce sriracha (Asian chili sauce)
½ pound fava beans, blanched and peeled
½ pound fresh Dungeness crabmeat

For green olive pesto:

¼ cup pitted Greek green olives
1 teaspoon chipotle peppers, reconstituted

Mix mustard seeds and ground mustard. Thoroughly coat all sides of ahi with mustard mix. Heat olive oil over medium-high heat. Sear tuna for 3 seconds on each side, to rare. Place on paper towels to remove excess oil. Set aside, keeping warm for final plating.

To make the salad, preheat oven to 350°F. Cut cauliflower into bite-size pieces, toss in olive oil, and lightly salt and pepper. Place on a baking sheet lined with wax paper and bake in the preheated oven for 20 minutes or until golden brown. Place in refrigerator to cool.

In a large bowl, mix mayonnaise, crème fraîche, chives, lemon juice, sriracha, and salt and pepper to taste. Add cauliflower, fava beans, and Dungeness crab and lightly toss until well incorporated.

To make the pesto, blend olives and chipotle peppers in a food processor until smooth.

To serve, place the cauliflower salad in the center of the plate. Slice tuna as desired and place on top of the cauliflower salad. Finish with a light drizzle of the green olive pesto and serve.

Silverado Resort & Spa

1600 Atlas Peak Road
Napa, CA 94558
(707) 257-0200
www.silveradoresort.com
Executive Chef: Jeffrey Jake

With its colonial style and gorgeous grounds, the Silverado Resort & Spa is a natural choice for special events and important occasions. Known for its PGA-level golfing and state-of-the-art spa facilities, now, with its new executive chef, Jeffrey Jake, the resort has reaffirmed its commitment to outstanding cuisine with its fine-dining venue: the Oak Room.

A Napa Valley native, Jake's father was chief of surgery at the Veterans Affairs hospital in Yountville, one of the oldest in the United States. Although he thought he'd follow his father's footsteps in the medical world, Jake discovered a love of cooking at his grandmother's house on her large farm in Wisconsin—and this became the deciding factor in his pursuit to become a chef.

His professional culinary career began in the pastry kitchen at Domaine Chandon, with revered Napa Valley chef Udo Nechutnys. Gradually, Jake made his way into the main kitchen at Chandon, with Nechutnys as a mentor, and became hooked on the work—both physically and mentally.

The two moved together up the valley to run the Miramonte Hotel in St. Helena, collecting incredible culinary experiences throughout that journey. Jake recalls cooking with live turtles and catching trout in the restaurant's pond for truite au bleu—where the fish is cooked immediately after being killed, in a boiling court-bouillon, giving its skin a unique metallic blue hue. They also handpicked roosters from a local farm for their coq au vin—catching them on-site with a burlap sack.

After stints at highly regarded restaurants in Monterey and Pacific Grove, Jake made his way back to the Napa Valley to be closer to family. He spent time at the Sonoma Mission Inn (page 94), Farm Restaurant, and the Carneros Inn before joining the team at Silverado.

All of this experience in some of California's finest restaurants has informed Jake's style of cuisine in wine country. He looks for flavor affinities shared between food and wine, and credits his time working on a crushpad with legendary regional chef and mentor John Ash for sharpening his pairing abilities and deepening his understanding of the marriage between wine and great cuisine. His diners' increasing sophistication continues to motivate his style of cuisine, best described as Mediterranean, featuring California ingredients and creative menus. Jake's vision is to create an extensive on-site farm, to not only enable access to the best local ingredients but also offer an educational component for guests and local children—on the benefits of healthy eating based on local, whole foods.

Line-Caught Pacific Swordfish with Salsa Verde

(SERVES 4)

For the salsa verde:

1 cup extra-virgin olive oil
Juice of 1 lemon
2 bunches Italian parsley, stems removed and leaves chopped
6 garlic cloves, minced
½ cup chopped basil
¼ cup chopped oregano
¼ teaspoon red wine vinegar
1 teaspoon chili flakes
3 shallots, diced
2 teaspoons sea salt

For the swordfish:

4 (7- to 8-ounce) swordfish steaks (1½ inches thick)
3 tablespoons olive oil
1 tablespoon sea salt
1 tablespoon fresh cracked black pepper
¼ cup salsa verde

Mix all the salsa verde ingredients together at least 2 hours before serving your meal. It must be made fresh each day. If desired, reserve the past day's salsa for use as a marinade.

Preheat oven to 450°F. Rub swordfish steaks with olive oil and season liberally with sea salt and fresh cracked pepper. Turn oven to broil.

Place swordfish on a perforated roasting pan or rack. Slide under the broiler on the top shelf and cook for about 4 minutes per side. (Chef Jake likes this method, as the fish retains more moisture.)

Remove swordfish to a warm plate and top with salsa verde. At the restaurant, they garnish with peppery watercress tossed with St. Helena Lemon Oil and fried onions.

Peruvian Chicken with Zucchini Spaghettini & Lime Aioli

(SERVES 6)

For the marinade:

1 cup champagne vinegar
¾ cup dry white wine
¾ cup extra-virgin olive oil
3 garlic cloves, lightly smashed
½ cup smoked paprika
1 tablespoon Marrakesh pepper
⅓ cup toasted cumin seeds
2 tablespoons cracked black pepper
1 tablespoon sea salt

For the chicken:

6 (10-ounce) portions chicken breast, organic preferred
¼ cup grapeseed oil

For the lime aioli:

1 cup mayonnaise
¼ cup Dijon mustard
¼ cup lime juice

For the zucchini salad:

4 medium zucchini
¼ cup crushed Marcona almonds
½ cup grated ricotta salata
1 teaspoon Meyer lemon zest
2 tablespoons Meyer lemon juice
½ cup extra-virgin olive oil
Sea salt and fresh ground pepper to taste

Combine the marinade ingredients into a paste and set aside. Trim, wash, and dry the chicken breast.

Rub the marinade paste into the chicken and under the skin. Place in a resealable plastic bag and marinate for 4–5 hours. Remove from marinade; rinse and pat dry. Discard marinade.

Preheat oven to 375°F. Pan-sear the chicken breasts skin-side down over medium heat in grapeseed oil, cooking until golden brown. Place in the preheated oven for approximately 12 minutes. Remove from oven and let rest 5 minutes before serving.

To make the aioli, mix the mayonnaise and Dijon mustard together. Stir in lime juice and check for seasoning. Serve on the side.

To make the salad, julienne the zucchini on a mandoline to create spaghetti strands of zucchini. Add crushed almonds, crumbled ricotta, and lemon zest and toss with the zucchini. Add lemon juice and olive oil and season with salt and pepper. You may adjust ingredients in proportion to your preference.

To serve, place the zucchini salad in the center of a large serving plate. Place spiced chicken breasts on top and serve lime aioli on the side.

COUNTY LINE

SWEET & SAVORY ENDINGS

Throughout Sonoma County and along its borders lay hundreds of farms, picturesque apple orchards, and vineyards, with coastal winds sweeping across the land from the west colliding with the strong heat of the valley. It's beautiful countryside, a bit slower and more relaxed than the rest of the region, and is known for some of the best artisanal products and foods around.

Full of small farms and small towns, this area (leading all the way to the Pacific Ocean) is an ideal place to go wine tasting and eating, no matter your palate tendencies. Originally settled by Russians at Fort Ross on Coast Highway 1 in the early 1800s, the area is now known for being home to some of the most impressive vineyards in wine country—with more than 250 wine estates spanning the Russian River and Alexander Valley appellations all the way to the Mayacamas Mountains. It also boasts some of the best poultry producers and dairy farmers in California, resulting in succulent organic chicken, lovely farm-fresh butter, and delightful sheep's, goat's, and cow's milk cheese craved throughout the Bay Area and across the country. Apple farms are plentiful as are crops of hops, helping to shape the great beers of the region.

And the area is diverse. Though "small town" is what most of the places we feature here have in common, each one is unique in its own way. Petaluma is affectionately known as "the egg basket of the world," and so has incredible eggs, chickens, and farm products of all kinds; both of its restaurants featured here are run by people whose own farms supply many of their ingredients. Artsy Sebastopol is quirky, has a sweet little central town plaza, and hosts an apple blossom festival each spring; its Hopmonk Tavern is the place to celebrate food and beer. The coastal village of Marshall is home to the oyster, clam, and mussel farms that the revered Hog Island harvests for its own plates of raw, baked, or grilled oysters, clam chowders, and steamed mussels, which are fiendishly gobbled up by fans throughout the region. Santa Rosa is like the big city among the small towns of the collection, home to the Charles M. Schulz Museum for fans of Charlie Brown and the Peanuts gang, as well as the celebrated John Ash & Co. restaurant and zazu restaurant + farm—a long-timer and newbie, respectively, to the world of fine dining and farm-to-table cooking.

Prepare to taste your way through the recipes offered by this incredible collection of chefs and restaurateurs—and imagine being surrounded by some of the most vibrant and delicious artisanal foods, winning praise from connoisseurs coast to coast, just as they are.

Central Market

42 Petaluma Boulevard
Petaluma, CA 94952
(707) 778-9900
www.centralmarketpetaluma.com
Chef/Owner: Tony Najiola

When he walks across the street from his restaurant to the local neighborhood cafe, chef Tony Najiola is like the mayor of the town. In the space of a single hour, he greets members of his staff, a revered legendary farmer who reportedly "never goes out," and countless friends and customers who seem to love him. Najiola, from New Orleans by way of New York and San Francisco, has worked for some of the most famous chefs in the world. But he is happiest now, in the small town of Petaluma, running his own restaurant, which he describes as having "the best location in town."

His food is accessible, delicious, and resists categories. Though he's a "Nawlander," there is no gumbo on his menu. He says he most treasures the warm hospitality and reverence for fine food that one finds in his hometown. He likes simple, straightforward preparations—and is moving even more toward simplicity as he works to showcase the fresh products (including pig) from his Muleheart Farm, just two miles away. Najiola works on his farm every morning and is completely at home there, naming it as he did "because you have to have the heart of a mule to own a restaurant and a farm." Even given this new labor-intensive project, Najiola is not missing a beat, and his largely Mediterranean flavor–focused restaurant is as delicious as ever.

Najiola makes a mean fried smelt, handles local fish and pork (much of it his own) beautifully, and treats classic dishes like steamed mussels with both reverence and fun—adding new spices for interest but not futzing too much with a classic. Central Market has an oyster bar, a lovely wine list hand-selected by Najiola himself, and an array of meats, poultry, fish, and pizzas fired in the restaurant's wood-burning oven.

The atmosphere is convivial, the space full of Petaluma locals eagerly tucking into Najiola's dinners every night of the week. Some even join to celebrate the holidays—the chef has offered a multicourse Thanksgiving dinner for the last eight years. Described by a friend as "Petaluma's restaurant—it is fresh, local and yummy," Central Market is, simply put, just that. It is a restaurant for the people, both locals and those just passing through town, and is always pretty darn yummy.

Summer Berries on Corn Flour Shortcakes

(YIELDS 8 SHORTCAKES)

For the shortcakes:

2 cups all-purpose flour, unbleached
¼ cup corn flour
2 teaspoons baking powder
¼ teaspoon baking soda
1 teaspoon salt
¼ cup sugar, divided
1½ cups heavy cream, as needed
1 egg (for egg wash)

For the berry garnish:

3 pints summer sweet berries
Sugar to taste
3 lemons, zest and juice

For the sweetened whipped cream:

2 cups heavy organic cream
2 tablespoons or more sugar to taste

To serve:

¼ cup butter, for brushing
¼ cup powdered sugar, for dusting

Mix flour with corn flour, baking powder, baking soda, salt, and half the sugar in a large bowl. Pour in cream to just moisten, stirring and kneading lightly only until flour is absorbed and dough adheres. Wrap in plastic and refrigerate 1 hour.

Preheat oven to 350°F. On a lightly floured surface, roll out dough until 2 inches thick, cut desired shapes, and place on a parchment-lined sheet pan. Brush with egg and sprinkle with remaining sugar. Bake in the preheated oven until golden brown, about 25 minutes.

To make the berry garnish, puree 1 pint of berries with sugar and lemon juice (from 1–2 lemons) to taste. You may wish to strain afterward to remove seeds. The remainder of berries can be halved, sliced, or left whole and are macerated with 3 tablespoons of berry puree, zest of 1 lemon, and juice of 1 lemon.

Combine the whipped cream ingredients. Whip until soft peaks are formed and refrigerate until needed. Re-whip a bit right before use.

To assemble, slice shortcakes in half, brush with butter, and warm in oven. When ready to plate, place a bit of cream on the plate and add bottom half of shortcake (cream keeps cake in place). Place 2 tablespoons of puree on bottom half and top with berries, more puree, and whipped cream. Moisten top half of shortcake with puree and place on top of the whipped cream (like a sandwich). Sprinkle with powdered sugar.

Della Fattoria

141 Petaluma Boulevard North
Petaluma, CA 94952
(707) 763-0161
www.dellafattoria.com
Owners/Operators: The Weber Family (Kathleen, Edmund, Elisa, and Aaron)

The bread of the storybooks, of history, and of the tales that shape our lives—this is the bread that Weber family matriarch, Kathleen, is drawn to. A true romantic when it comes to bread, Kathleen was first influenced by Carol Field's lauded 1985 book, *The Italian Baker,* which became a classic for subsequent generations, and started baking bread at home for the family. Family dinners became extended dinner parties, and the dinner parties turned into a catering operation. Gradually the Weber family bread became a business, and in 2004 the business became a storefront, in a bakery and cafe now called Della Fattoria. Meaning "of the farm," Della Fattoria reflects the fact that all of the breads, pastries, and dishes come in some way from their nearby family ranch, many baked in the wood-burning oven there.

The Webers are consummate entertainers—they even welcome educational field trips and overnight guests at their farm—and this sensibility permeates their homey bakery-cafe. With communal tables that run along either side of the restaurant and a

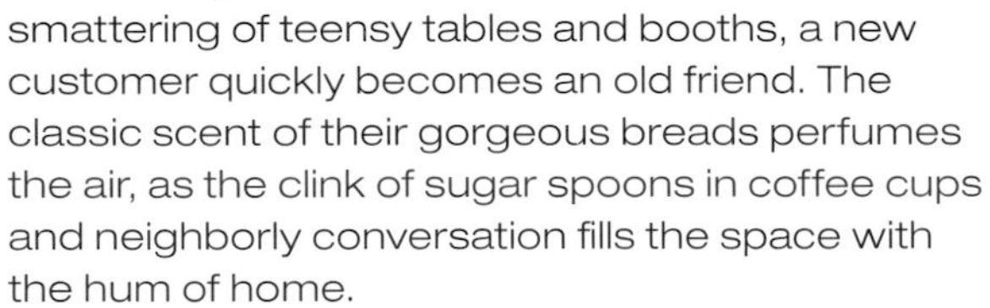

smattering of teensy tables and booths, a new customer quickly becomes an old friend. The classic scent of their gorgeous breads perfumes the air, as the clink of sugar spoons in coffee cups and neighborly conversation fills the space with the hum of home.

But about that bread: It is truly something special. The family's famous rosemary–Meyer lemon loaves fly off the shelves daily, and the inspiration behind the bread, not surprisingly, comes from history. Kathleen describes a classic Medici tale wherein the royal baker makes a round loaf, its top heavily sprinkled with coarse salt to "sparkle like diamonds." And lightly toasted, spread with a thick puree of the locally famous Rancho Gordo cannellini beans, blended with chèvre, garlic, and olive oil, it is downright addictive—easily enjoyed at any time of day. Naturally, the sweet pastries are also amazing, ranging from éclairs and rustic tarts to classic home-style cakes and traditional Italian favorites.

Kathleen and Edmund have successfully involved both of their children in the business over the years. Their son, Aaron, a talented chef in his

own right, organized their production baking years ago and helped design the menu, and daughter Elisa, a photographer and talented woodworker (she made all of the cafe's tables herself), runs the operation today.

"The baker was always the center of the community," Kathleen explains, discussing her love of bread and the family's vision for the business. Nothing is fancy or contrived at Della Fattoria—"it's not our style." And, just as tradition dictates, this baker—and bakery—is at the heart of the community.

Caramel Ice Box Cake

(SERVES 6)

At Della Fattoria, this has become one of everybody's favorite desserts.

For the caramel sauce:

1½ cups heavy cream
1 cup sugar
½ cup corn syrup
2 tablespoons butter, room temperature
1 teaspoon vanilla extract

For the filling and to assemble the cake:

½ pound cream cheese, room temperature
¼ cup sugar
2¼ cups heavy cream
1 tablespoon strong coffee
2 tablespoons amaretto liqueur
¾ cup caramel sauce
12–15 crisp chocolate chip cookies, broken into 1-inch pieces if they are larger then the ramekin

To make the caramel sauce, bring the cream to a boil in a small saucepan, then turn the burner off. Cover to retain the heat and set aside.

In a heavy-bottomed saucepan, combine the sugar and corn syrup and set over medium heat. Cook, stirring periodically until the sugar has dissolved. Stop stirring and cook until it turns a golden color, swirling if the color is not even throughout.

Remove from heat and add the butter in small chunks, stirring. Carefully stir in the hot cream, mixing until fully incorporated. Transfer to a heatproof container or bowl and allow to cool to room temperature before adding the vanilla extract. (This will make more than what is needed, but it keeps for up to 6 weeks in an airtight container; keep refrigerated.)

To make to the filling, combine cream cheese, sugar, heavy cream, coffee, and amaretto in the bowl of an electric mixer with the whisk attachment. Slowly increase the speed until soft peaks form. Slowly add the caramel sauce down the side of the bowl and continue mixing until stiff peaks form.

To assemble the cake, place a single layer of cookies into each ramekin. Spoon 3 tablespoons of filling over the cookies and spread to cover the cookies. Repeat the layer 2 more times, finishing with a layer of cream. Cover each ramekin with plastic wrap and refrigerate for at least 8 hours, preferably overnight.

To serve, drizzle the top of each ramekin with some of the extra caramel and garnish with chocolate shavings or extra cookie pieces.

Walnut Torte

(SERVES 8)

This recipe comes from Kathleen's grandmother.

For the torte:

½ cup butter
½ cup sugar
4 egg yolks
1½ teaspoons vanilla extract
1 cup cake flour
2 teaspoons baking powder
5 tablespoons milk
1 cup walnuts, coarsely chopped

For the meringue:

4 egg whites
1 cup sugar

Preheat oven to 375°F.

In the bowl of an electric mixer with the paddle attachment, cream the butter and sugar until light and fluffy. Add the egg yolks one at a time, mixing thoroughly after each addition. Mix in the vanilla.

In a small bowl, sift together the cake flour and baking powder. Alternately mix together the flour mixture and the milk, starting and ending with the flour.

Spread the batter in a 9½- x 1½-inch round baking dish and evenly sprinkle the chopped walnuts on top. Bake for 20 minutes.

During the last 5 minutes of baking, prepare the meringue. In a bowl of an electric mixer with the whisk attachment, whip the egg whites on high speed until frothy. With the mixer running, slowly add the sugar and beat until the meringue is thick and shiny.

Spread the meringue over the cake and continue baking for 35–45 minutes, until the meringue has an even golden color throughout. Serve warm with berries.

Almond Blackberry Coeur a la Crème

(SERVES 6)

For the blackberry sauce:

1 pint blackberries
¼–⅓ cup sugar
Juice of ½ lemon

For the coeur a la crème:

1 cup mascarpone, room temperature
½ cup sugar
1 teaspoon orange zest
½ teaspoon almond extract
2 cups cold heavy cream
½ cup blackberries, cut in half
Sliced almonds for garnish

To make the blackberry sauce, combine all the ingredients in a medium saucepan over medium-low heat. Using a fork or a small whisk, break up the blackberries. Cook for 10–12 minutes, until the sauce starts to thicken slightly. This sauce is great slightly warm or at room temperature.

To make the coeur a la crème, in the bowl of an electric mixer fitted with the whisk attachment, whisk mascarpone and sugar along with the orange zest until light and fluffy. Add the almond extract followed by the cream and whisk on high speed until soft peaks form. Gently fold in the blackberry halves.

Line 6 coeur a la crème molds with cheesecloth (with at least a 1-inch overhang) and evenly divide the cream. Turn over the extra cheesecloth to cover the top. Place the filled molds on a sheet pan, cover with plastic wrap, and allow to drain overnight in the fridge.

To serve, turn over each heart onto a dessert plate. Drizzle with the blackberry sauce and sprinkle with sliced almonds.

Hopmonk Tavern

230 Petaluma Avenue
Sebastopol, CA 95472
(707) 829-7300

691 Broadway
Sonoma, CA 95476
(707) 935-9100
www.hopmonk.com
Owner: Dean Biersch; Executive Chef: Billy Reid

Beer can be as complex as wine, if not more, says Billy Reid, executive "rock star" chef—his actual title, and he looks every bit the part—of Hopmonk Tavern, with locations in both Sebastopol and Sonoma. Though he was born in Virginia Beach, Reid describes himself as from Las Vegas, the place where he worked early on as a musician and, in the process, became a chef. He took a job in a kitchen to supplement his gig earnings and gradually saw a future in food.

Though he quickly got accustomed to serving thousands of people a day in Vegas—with pallets of the finest halibut—it was in Sonoma where he saw his first whole, un-filleted salmon.

"They don't call it 'Slow-noma' for nothing," Reid says, referring to both the city and the county. "People take their time here with food." And though he loves the fast pace of Vegas, "simplicity is how I roll," claims the rock star chef, describing his style of cooking. On average, his dishes feature only five to eight ingredients apiece.

It seems a perfect match for the brewpub launched by beer royalty, Dean Biersch, half of the Gordon Biersch brewery-restaurant empire. Hopmonk features live music at both locations and boasts a "beer bible" for perusing its more than one hundred brews, about a dozen or so of which are typically on tap.

Reid and his team also organize regular "brewmaster dinners" in partnership with local beermakers to broaden the spotlight beyond Hopmonk's own creations to the diverse array of other brews that hail from the Bay Area. Menus for these affairs naturally highlight what is special about each beer, while also evoking Reid's fun, eclectic, and surreptitiously classical style of cooking. In one dinner, he started with a "chocolate-dusted mango pops" pairing and offered coconut-crusted halibut with garam masala as a main. But he'd just as easily and happily make something like the tavern-style bread pudding or beer and cheese fondue (both featured here).

It should also be noted that Reid is a certified specialist of wine—a distinction that shows a level of mastery about aspects of viticulture and wine production. Don't let his rock star image fool you: This guy knows his stuff when it comes to food and wine, and, of course, beer.

Beer & Cheese Fondue

(YIELD 2 QUARTS)

This dish is for the savory lovers.

1 cup butter, unsalted
½ cup finely diced red onion
Pinch of chili pepper flakes
½ cup all-purpose flour, plus a little more as needed
1 pint light ale (such as Hopmonk Tavern Ale, Smithwick's, Anchor Liberty, etc.)
1 quart (4 cups) heavy cream
½ cup sharp yellow cheddar cheese, shredded
½ cup mild white cheddar cheese, shredded
½ cup Swiss cheese, shredded
¼ cup lemon juice
Salt and pepper to taste
Assorted fresh breads and crostini to serve

In a large pot over medium-high heat, add butter and melt until it is almost brown. Add onions and chili pepper flakes and cook until onions are translucent.

To the onion-butter mixture, whisk in the flour to make a roux (a classic thickening base of flour and butter, cooked to varying stages of golden through dark brown, depending on the recipe or cuisine). Continue cooking, stirring constantly with a wooden spoon, until the roux reaches the brown stage. This should take several minutes.

Add the beer, stirring the mixture until it becomes smooth, then add all the cream and continue stirring until the sauce is homogenous. Reduce temperature to a simmer and add the cheeses slowly, continuing to stir until all cheese is thoroughly blended into the mixture.

Add the lemon juice, continuing to stir, and season with salt and pepper. Bring up temperature slightly to a low heat and continue stirring the mixture until it is thick enough to coat the back of the spoon ("nappe"). Serve warm, with assorted breads.

Tavern-Style Bread Pudding with Whiskey & Brown Sugar Sauce

(SERVES 8)

For the bread pudding:

8 eggs
4 cups sugar, divided
1 pint cream
1½ teaspoons nutmeg
½ teaspoon salt
1 pound unsalted butter, softened to room temperature
2 loaves or equivalent of bread (such as potato, sour, or classic white), sliced and crusts removed

For the brown sugar sauce:

1 pint heavy cream
1 cup dark brown sugar
1 cup butter
2 tablespoons lemon juice
Pinch of kosher salt

For the whiskey sauce:

1 quart (4 cups) cream
1 cup unsalted butter
6 egg yolks
1 cup sugar
Pinch of salt
1 cup whiskey

Preheat oven to 375°F.

In a large bowl, crack all of the eggs and add 2 cups of sugar. Whisk until the eggs thicken and the mixture flows off of the whisk slowly (this is called the "ribbons stage"). Add the cream, nutmeg, and salt and whisk to combine.

Blend the softened butter with the remaining 2 cups of sugar. Spread this butter-sugar mixture on the sliced bread to create "bread and butter" sandwiches. Cut sandwiches into small strips or dice. Place the sandwich strips or cubes into another large bowl.

Slowly add the egg and cream mixture to the bowl of "sandwiches" and combine by hand. You're looking for an oatmeal-like consistency. Go slowly.

Place the mixture in a single large casserole dish or several large ovenproof cups or ramekins. Place in a water bath and bake, covered, for 15–20 minutes. Uncover and cook for an additional 10 minutes or until golden brown.

To make the brown sugar sauce, bring cream to a simmer in a large saucepan over medium-high heat. Upon the simmer, add brown sugar, butter, lemon juice, and salt; bring back to a simmer and whisk to combine. Remove from heat and set aside.

To make the whiskey sauce, bring cream and butter to a simmer in a large saucepot over medium-high heat. Meanwhile, in another large saucepot, whisk egg yolks, sugar, salt, and whiskey together until homogenous. Temper hot cream-butter mixture into egg mixture, very slowly and stirring constantly. Continue cooking over medium heat and continue whisking until sauce starts to thicken. Remove from heat and hold in warm water.

To plate the bread pudding, cut individual servings from the casserole dish, or serve individual ramekin portions. Spoon a bit of the brown sugar and whiskey sauces over the top of each portion, to taste.

John Ash & Co.

4330 Barnes Road
Santa Rosa, CA 95403
(707) 527-7687
www.vintnersinn.com/dining
Chef: Tom Schmidt; Pastry Chef: Casey Stone

The namesake of legendary wine country chef John Ash, the John Ash & Co. restaurant at the Vintners Inn in Santa Rosa simply drips with the region's culinary history.

"Wine country cuisine came very naturally. It has always been about great local seasonal foods with an eye to the marriage of wine," says Ash, who founded the restaurant in 1980. And after four cookbooks, a more than twenty-year-long radio program that's still on the air, various food TV shows, thousands of classes and consulting gigs, and an ongoing blog, he remains an important figure in wine country cuisine to this day.

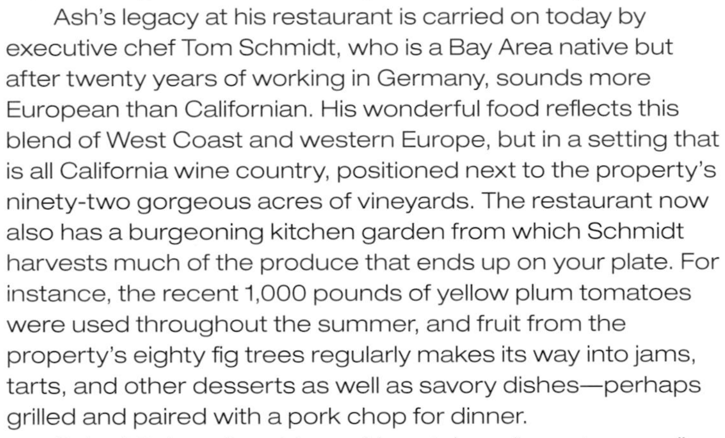

Ash's legacy at his restaurant is carried on today by executive chef Tom Schmidt, who is a Bay Area native but after twenty years of working in Germany, sounds more European than Californian. His wonderful food reflects this blend of West Coast and western Europe, but in a setting that is all California wine country, positioned next to the property's ninety-two gorgeous acres of vineyards. The restaurant now also has a burgeoning kitchen garden from which Schmidt harvests much of the produce that ends up on your plate. For instance, the recent 1,000 pounds of yellow plum tomatoes were used throughout the summer, and fruit from the property's eighty fig trees regularly makes its way into jams, tarts, and other desserts as well as savory dishes—perhaps grilled and paired with a pork chop for dinner.

Schmidt describes his cooking style as "spontaneous" and based on fresh ingredients, essentially farm-to-table. His secret "Bonsai menu" is available by prior arrangement, for those in the know, and features eight to ten courses, all small plates, to highlight the best seasonal ingredients and enable Schmidt an outlet for whimsy and the spontaneity he so enjoys. After more than thirty years of cooking, he says he can't think of anything else he'd rather do.

His pastry chef, Casey Stone, feels similarly. Born and raised on the big island of Hawaii, Stone first fell in love with bread and desserts during his initial culinary program straight out of high school at Le Cordon Bleu in Portland, Oregon. After working in fine dining and finishing a second culinary stint at The Culinary Institute of America in St. Helena, Stone is at home in pastry. "I love being able to be creative, continuously learning, exciting all of my senses, and most importantly, satisfying the heck out of my sweet tooth," he says. The following recipes from Stone are sure to do just that for you too.

Limoncello Fromage Blanc Cheesecake

(SERVES 8)

For the gingersnap crust:

1 cup crushed gingersnap cookies
3 tablespoons butter, melted

For the filling:

1 pound fromage blanc
1 pound cream cheese (one that contains no stabilizers or gums)
12 ounces superfine sugar
Zest of 1 lemon
1 tablespoon limoncello
2 eggs
¼ teaspoon vanilla bean paste

For the passion fruit consommé:

2 cups unsweetened passion fruit juice
1 cup orange juice
½ cup superfine sugar
2 tablespoons cornstarch
2 tablespoons water

To serve:

Coconut sorbet

To make the crust, preheat oven to 300°F. Line an 18- x 13-inch pan (half sheet pan) with parchment paper. Place 8 3-inch-wide individual rings on pan. Mix crushed gingersnaps with butter and divide evenly among rings. Press down firmly with a wooden dowel or a tart tamper. Bake for 10 minutes. Remove and cool.

To make the filling, mix fromage blanc and cream cheese in a standing mixer bowl, using the paddle attachment on low speed for 8 minutes. Stop and scrape down bowl with a rubber spatula. On low speed, slowly add sugar and continue mixing. This should take around 5 minutes. Stop and scrape down bowl. Still on low speed, add the rest of the ingredients and mix until smooth. Divide into rings and bake until top is set and jiggles slightly, around 30–40 minutes. Chill in refrigerator until cold.

To remove from rings, use a small kitchen torch and lightly hit the sides of the ring; tap on a plate until cheesecake is released.

To make the consommé, heat passion fruit juice, orange juice, and sugar in a small saucepan. In a small bowl, whisk cornstarch and water until well combined. When juice comes to a boil, slowly whisk into cornstarch. Add back to the saucepan and bring back to a boil. Continue cooking for 1 minute. Pour into a bowl and chill in refrigerator until cold.

Serve the cheesecake with the passion fruit consommé and coconut sorbet.

Sonoma Blackout Cake

(SERVES 6)

For the cake:

1½ cup plus 1½ tablespoons all-purpose flour
¾ cup high-quality cocoa powder
1 teaspoon baking powder
2 teaspoons baking soda
½ teaspoon kosher salt
1 tablespoon fresh lemon juice
¾ cup plus 3 tablespoons whole milk
2 eggs, room temperature
2 cups superfine sugar
½ cup canola oil
1 cup strong brewed coffee
¾ teaspoon vanilla extract
¼ teaspoon almond extract

For the pudding:

1 egg, room temperature
1 egg yolk, room temperature
1½ cup whole milk
⅓ cup superfine sugar
¼ teaspoon salt
2 tablespoons high-quality cocoa powder
1 tablespoon plus 1 teaspoon cornstarch
4 ounces bittersweet chocolate, finely chopped
1½ tablespoons butter
1 tablespoon amaretto

For the top of the cake:

1 box chocolate wafer cookies, crushed finely in food processor

For the vanilla-orange stewed cherries:

2 cups frozen sour cherries
½ cup superfine sugar
2 teaspoons balsamic vinegar
1 teaspoon vanilla bean paste
Zest of 1 orange
¼ cup red wine

To serve:

Vanilla gelato
Chocolate cookies

Preheat oven to 350°F. Line an 18- x 13-inch pan (half sheet pan) with a piece of parchment paper to fit on the bottom of the pan.

Sift flour, cocoa, baking powder, baking soda, and salt in a medium-size bowl. In a separate bowl, mix lemon juice and milk together and let stand for 5 minutes.

Place eggs and sugar in a standing mixer bowl. Using the paddle attachment, mix until eggs are a pale yellow and mixture is thickened. Add canola oil to egg mixture on slow speed. Slowly add the sifted dry ingredients, alternating with the soured milk. Add coffee and extracts and mix until batter just comes together.

Pour batter into the prepared pan and bake until a toothpick inserted into the center of the cake comes out clean, about 25 minutes. Let cake cool completely.

To make the pudding, mix egg and egg yolk in a small bowl and set aside. Heat milk over low heat in a saucepan.

In a bowl, whisk sugar, salt, cocoa, and cornstarch. Slowly whisk a little of the hot milk into the cocoa mixture to make a paste, then slowly mix in the rest of the hot milk.

Pour the mixture back into the saucepan and cook over low heat until it comes to a boil. Continuously whisk and cook for 1 minute. Slowly temper in egg and egg yolk. Cook for 30 seconds, then strain over a bowl containing the chocolate and butter. Whisk together and add amaretto. Place a piece of plastic wrap directly on the surface and place in refrigerator to cool completely.

To assemble, remove the cake from the pan and slice crosswise into 3 pieces. Remove parchment from the bottom of the cake. Spread a third of the pudding on one layer of cake. Continue layering with cake and pudding until you finish with a layer of pudding on top. Top cake with crushed chocolate wafer cookies, then wrap cake in plastic and chill until ready to serve.

To make the stewed cherries, mix all of the ingredients in a saucepan and cook until mixture comes to a boil. Strain out cherries and reserve in a small bowl. Bring mixture back to a boil and cook for 3 minutes until mixture slightly reduces. Remove orange zest and pour over reserved cherries; chill in refrigerator until cold.

Cut the cake crosswise into 6 pieces. Serve with the vanilla-orange stewed cherries, vanilla gelato, and a chocolate cookie of your choice.

ZAZU RESTAURANT + FARM

3535 Guerneville Road
Santa Rosa, CA 95401
(707) 523-4814
www.zazurestaurant.com
Chefs/Owners: Duskie Estes
and John Stewart

You may have seen her on TV. Or you may have tried their bacon. If you've known nothing about Duskie Estes or John Stewart until now, be certain of this: They exemplify in just about every way the commitment to local products, eating well, and having a connection to your food that so many people pontificate about today. This married couple runs a fabulous restaurant in an unexpected spot on a country highway in Sonoma County, and once you eat there, you will want to be a regular, take their cooking classes, and pick from their vegetable garden.

Estes and Stewart, who also run zazu on the river, in Healdsburg (page 34), met in Seattle while working together at a restaurant by acclaimed Pacific Northwest chef Tom Douglas. And it wasn't mutual love at first sight.

"I was his boss—and had a crush on him, but it took him a little longer," Estes explains. Now, they have two kids, two restaurants, a line of bacon, and umpteen animals on their home farm, including dogs, cats, chickens, goats, rabbits, sheep, pigs, a hamster and a rescued rooster. MacBryde Farm, named for their daughters, Mackenzie and Brydie, provides many of the restaurant's ingredients.

In 2009 Estes competed on the Food Network's *The Next Iron Chef* after never having seen the show before—the couple does not own a TV. She did it for the restaurant and to bring attention to the couple's passion for respecting your food source.

She describes their food at zazu as "playful Americana" and rustic northern Italian inspired. The kitchen emphasizes ingredients grown within fifty miles of the restaurant—some of them come from as close as fifty feet away.

Exactly what you'd imagine when you think "roadside diner," but elegant, comforting, and homey all at the same time, zazu is home to Monday-night farm dinners, Sunday brunch, "Pizza and Pinot" two nights a week, and dinner five nights a week. The team even features a "you-pick" item, offering diners an opportunity to hand-select their own squash blossoms or other lovely vegetable from the restaurant's garden troughs to appear on their plate a few minutes later. Even the desserts at this family affair deliver a delicious, homegrown experience.

Redwood Hill Goat Yogurt Panna Cotta with Red Wine Blueberry Sauce

(SERVES 14)

For the panna cotta:

2⅔ cups heavy cream
1 cup sugar
Pinch of dried lavender
1 lemon, zested
4 gelatin sheets (available at www.chefshop.com), or substitute 1 packet gelatin
1 quart (4 cups) plain goat yogurt
Nonstick spray

For the blueberry sauce:

½ cup red wine
½ cup sugar
1 teaspoon lemon juice
1 teaspoon vanilla extract
2 pints blueberries

Prepare the ramekins with nonstick spray.

In a heavy-bottomed saucepan, on medium heat, combine the heavy cream, sugar, lavender, and lemon zest. Stir occasionally until sugar is melted.

Pour mixture over gelatin sheets to soften and melt, stirring. (If substituting a gelatin packet, soften the gelatin with ⅔ cup of the cream in a small bowl. Heat the remainder of the cream with sugar, lavender, and lemon in a sauce pan.) Pour through a sieve to remove lavender and zest. Whisk in the yogurt. Pour into prepared ramekins and let set in refrigerator a few hours or overnight.

To make the sauce, combine the red wine, sugar, and lemon juice in a small saucepan on medium-high heat. Bring to a simmer until thickened like maple syrup, about 5 minutes. Add the vanilla and blueberries. (This is also great on pancakes and waffles!)

To serve, "tickle" the edges of each panna cotta and turn them out. Serve each with spoonful of blueberry sauce.

Backyard Raspberry + Russian River Pinot Noir Sorbet in a Honey Cone

(SERVES 8)

The pinot noir out of the Russian River Valley is phenomenal. We made this sorbet to show it off. As for the honey cone, we are on a mission to support local honey with the bee crisis. Did you know 75 percent of the food on our dinner plate depends on pollination?

For the honey cones:

¼ cup unsalted butter, soft
2 tablespoons local honey (zazu prefers Hector's)
½ cup flour
½ cup powdered sugar
1 egg white
Pinch of lavender

For the sorbet:

1 pint raspberries
1 cup sugar
1 cup pinot noir
2 cups water

Preheat oven to 375°F.

In an electric mixer with the paddle attachment, beat the butter and honey until combined. Sift the flour and powdered sugar into the butter mixture and mix until smooth. Beat in the egg white until just combined.

Using a silpat, spread tablespoons of the batter into circles about 6 inches in diameter. Sprinkle each tuile with a tiny bit of lavender. Bake until golden on the edges, about 7 minutes. Work quickly to form the cones using a cone dowel. (Or you can make into other desired shapes.)

To make the sorbet, combine the raspberries, sugar, wine, and water in a small saucepan over medium-high heat and simmer for 15 minutes. Strain, cool, and freeze according to your ice cream machine's directions.

BELLWETHER FARMS

PO Box 299, Valley Ford, CA 94972
(707) 478-8067 · www.bellwetherfarms.com
Owners: Cindy and Liam Callahan

"The unlikely cheesemaker," Cindy Callahan founded her Sonoma farm in the early 1980s as part of a deliberate choice to change her lifestyle from what was a comfortable life in the nearby city of San Francisco. From that simple decision, Callahan has helped revolutionize cheesemaking in her region, building a truly unique, family-run business over the years, where a connection with the animals—and a conviction to produce the best local cheese—is at the heart of the operation.

She says of that time in her life that she felt she needed to "connect with the land" and feel grounded, and the farm, especially the presence of the sheep, provided that comfort. Soon there were more sheep in the field than she could admittedly handle.

Fortuitously, at the same time there was a surge of chefs in the region—and many of them sought whole baby lamb for their craft. "We took special pride in the quality of our lamb, and most of the top chefs of the region would track us down and ask us for our animals," she recalls. But they then had another issue: What to do with all the milk?

Callahan explains that they wanted to better understand the craft of cheesemaking, so they learned the best way they thought possible: at several fromageries in Italy.

A "life-changing experience," this formative time is what Callahan credits with her understanding of terroir and climate. She learned that cheese got its flavor from the grass the animals ate, and that seasonal changes brought out different nuances in that flavor. "The connection was enlightening," she shares.

After Italy, Callahan and her family decided the farm's new focus would be cheese. They'd realized the Sonoma climate and land was perfectly suited to crafting products they could be proud of—and so a legend in local cheesemaking was born.

Her son, Liam, who had been a political economy major at the University of California at Berkeley, played an important role in the farm's growing success, and his passion for the art of cheesemaking gradually led him to take over production. The farm now produces sheep's and cow's milk cheeses, along with yogurts, ricotta, and fromage blanc of amazing quality. His mother marvels at watching her son work the dairy floor, cutting warm curds, or washing cheese in the aging rooms—or even discussing with the farm team to which pastures the sheep should be moved—making clear the strong generational quality of this special business.

"I never suspected that I would become a farmer, but in reflection, our families were meant to work this land," Callahan shares. "It has been inspiring, and I'm so grateful for this journey."

Bellwether's many patrons at local farmers' markets as well as chefs across the country are grateful, too. The farm's lamb and many cheeses are in huge demand—and when you get on Bellwether's list of chefs, you know you are associated with something special.

Recipe Index

General Index

About the Authors

A California native drawn by centuries of history and culinary tradition, culinary director, chef, and author Roy Breiman moved to France, where he lived for several years. During his time there, he worked in kitchens of many Michelin-starred restaurants, primarily in Nice and Eze Village on the Côte d'Azur. He went on to work for five years as the Executive Chef at Meadowood Resort in Napa Valley. He is also owner of The West Coast Kitchen LLC, where he is providing counsel to a variety of groups on sustainable food concepts. In 1995 Breiman became a member of the James Beard Foundation. PBS named Breiman one of "America's Rising Star Chefs," John Mariani of *Esquire* magazine named him a "Chef to Keep Your Eyes On," and *Bon Appétit* magazine named him one of 13 "Top Hotel Chefs in America." Breiman also serves on the board of the Puget Sound Regional Food Council, helping to strengthen sustainable food systems and policies for the Puget Sound region. He lives in North Bend, Washington, with his wife, Pam, and golden retriever, Prince.

With a childhood search for the perfect chocolate mousse in her native Northern California, Laura Smith Borrman's food love started early. That love led to stints as a dessert caterer, baker, and culinary travel promoter in Chicago—followed by time as a pastry cook and hospitality writer in Seattle. A graduate from the master's program in international relations at the University of Chicago, Borrman's extensive writing experience spans work for major corporations, the hospitality industry, and public radio. She has interviewed many notable figures, including screen legend Julie Andrews, celebrity chef Charlie Trotter, beloved morning personality Matt Lauer, and entertainment icon William Shatner. She lives in Oakland, California, with her husband, Brandon, and their terrier mutt, Finnegan—and when she's not dining in California's wine country, she writes for her blog, cravingsofhome.com.